Paper 1

Energy

Energy changes in a system, and the ways energy is stored before and after such changes

Energy stores and systems

When there is a physical change to a system there is a change in the way energy is being stored.

1 There are three processes that cause changes in the way energy is stored in a system. Complete the table to give an example of each of the processes. One has been completed for you. **4 marks**

Process	Example	What would increase the energy change?
Heating		
Work being done by a force		
Work being done by an electric current	When an electric current powers an electric motor that lifts an object.	Increasing the height the object is lifted through or the weight of the object lifted.

2 Draw lines to link each description of how energy is stored with the equation that allows you to calculate the amount of energy in that store. **4 marks**

Description of energy store		Equation
The energy stored by an object off the ground in a gravitational field		$E_k = \frac{1}{2} m v^2$
The energy stored by a moving object		$E_p = m g h$
The energy store that changes when the temperature of an object changes		$E_e = \frac{1}{2} k e^2$
The energy stored when a material is stretched or compressed		$\Delta E = m c \Delta \theta$

Changes in energy

The set of energy equations can be used to calculate changes in systems because the total amount of energy is always conserved.

3 The table below shows a student's attempt to rearrange some energy equations using the standard set of symbols. The 'original equations' are correct. Cross out the incorrect rearrangements to leave only the correct ones. **3 marks**

Original equation			
$E_p = m g h$	$h = E_p m g$	$h = \dfrac{E_p}{m g}$	$m = \dfrac{E_p}{h g}$
$\Delta E = m c \Delta \theta$	$\Delta \theta = \dfrac{\Delta E}{m c}$	$\Delta \theta = \dfrac{m}{\Delta E c}$	$c = \dfrac{\Delta E}{m \Delta \theta}$
$E_k = \frac{1}{2} m v^2$	$v^2 = \dfrac{2 E_k}{m}$	$v = \dfrac{2 E_k}{m}$	$v = \sqrt[2]{\dfrac{2 E_k}{m}}$

Questions marked **1** **1** are for GCSE Physics students only

4 Match the quantity, symbol and correct unit by drawing lines. One has been done for you.

Quantity		Unit		Symbol
mass		J		e
speed		N/kg		k
energy		°C		m
temperature change		kg		g
spring constant		m		v
gravitational field strength		m/s		E
extension		N/m		$\Delta\theta$

Energy changes in systems

When the temperature of an object is increased, the energy stored thermally by the object also increases.

The amount of energy stored thermally is given by the equation:

change in thermal energy = mass × specific heat capacity × temperature change

_____ ____ _____ _____

5 Use the space underneath the equation above to write the correct units for each of the four variables.

6 When objects at different temperatures are placed in contact their temperature changes as energy is transferred. Describe what happens to the temperature of the object in the tables below. The start of some of the descriptions have been completed for you.

	A small metal block with a temperature of 200°C is placed in a large bowl of water with a temperature of 10°C.	An ice cube is placed in a warm beaker.
What happens to the temperature of the objects?	• The temperature of the metal block .... • The temperature of the water	
What happens to the thermal energy of the objects?	• The amount of thermal energy in the metal block	

Questions marked **1** **1** are for Combined Science Trilogy and GCSE Physics students

Power

The 'power' of a device is the rate at which it able to 'do work' (move an object using a force) or transfer energy by processes such as heating.

power = $\dfrac{\text{energy transferred}}{\text{time}}$ or $P = \dfrac{E}{t}$	power = $\dfrac{\text{work done}}{\text{time}}$ or $P = \dfrac{W}{t}$

7 Complete this sentence about the definition of power. Include suitable symbols for any units. **3 marks**

An energy transfer of 1 .... (.................) per .... (.................) is

equal to a power of .... (.................).

8 Rank the following in order from highest power (1) to lowest power (4). **4 marks**

Rank:	Rank:	Rank:	Rank: ....
Work done: 4000 J Time taken: 20 s	Work done: 3000 J Time taken: 10 s	Work done: 13 000 J Time taken: 1 minute	Work done: 15 kJ Time taken: 2 minutes

9 Complete this table about work done and power using the equations. Don't forget to add the units for work done and power. For this activity use gravitational field strength = 10 N/kg. **5 marks**

Work done (.................)	Time taken (s)	Power (.................)
12	20	0.6
10	10	
	40	20
600		30

Conservation and dissipation of energy

Energy transfers in a system

Energy can be transferred from one store to another but cannot be created or destroyed. In many transfers energy is transferred to thermal stores and becomes less useful; the energy is dissipated (spread out). Thermal energy transfers are reduced by using insulating materials.

10 Complete this sentence. **3 marks**

Energy losses from houses can be reduced by using thermal .... To reduce losses in

engines a ...., such as oil, can be used which reduces .... forces.

Efficiency

The efficiency of an energy transfer depends on how much energy is transferred in a useful way (useful energy) and how much energy is transferred in total.

11 Complete this table using the efficiency relationship. **4 marks**

Total energy input	Useful energy output	Efficiency	Efficiency %
500 J	325 J		
4.0 kJ			40%

National and global energy resources

We use a large number of energy resources each of which has advantages and disadvantages, including environmental impacts.

12 Complete this table showing some details of different energy resources. **19 marks**

Type of fuel	Renewable (R) or non-renewable (N)	Major use: transport (T) electricity generation (E) heating houses (H)	Reliability: very reliable (R) less reliable (U)	Example of negative impact or cost
Fossil fuel	N	T E H	R	
				Highly radioactive waste produced. Expensive to decommission.
	R	T E	U	Land could be used for food production instead.
				Visually unpleasant, sometimes noisy.
	R			Floods large areas of land.
Geothermal	R	E H	R	
	R	E	U	Can damage wildlife in estuaries.
Solar power				Expensive to build. Works best in sunny countries.
	R	E	U	Can block shipping lanes, very expensive.

Exam-style questions ⏲ 40

13 A gymnast jumps off a balance bar and lands on a crashmat. Complete the sentence below to describe the energy transfers. Use answers from these boxes. **3 marks**

> kinetic   sound   thermal   elastic potential   gravitational potential

While the gymnast stands on the balance bar she has a store of .... energy. As

she falls her store of .... energy increases. When the crashmat is squashed as

she lands the mat stores energy as .... energy.

Questions marked **1** **1** are for Combined Science Trilogy and GCSE Physics students

14 During an athletic event a javelin of mass 0.80 kg is thrown across a field and it follows a curved path. At the highest point of its flight the javelin reaches a height of 20 m and is travelling with a speed of 25 m/s.

The gravitational field strength is 9.8 N/kg.

a Calculate the gravitational potential energy of the javelin when it is at its highest point. *2 marks*

b Calculate the kinetic energy of the javelin at its highest point. *2 marks*

c What is the total energy stored by the javelin at its highest point. *1 mark*

d Explain what happens to this energy as the javelin hits the ground. *3 marks*

15 A spring is used to fire a stone vertically up into the air. The stone has a mass of 0.10 kg and leaves the catapult with a velocity of 4.0 m/s. The stone travels upwards until it reaches a maximum height and then falls back down to the ground.

The gravitational field strength is 9.8 N/kg.

a Calculate the kinetic energy of the stone as it left the catapult. *2 marks*

b What is the gain in gravitational potential energy as the stone reaches its maximum height? *1 mark*

c The spring used to launch the stone was compressed by 20 cm. Calculate its spring constant. *3 marks*

16 A cyclist is travelling along a flat, straight road at a constant speed. The cyclist sees a hazard and brakes, coming to a stop quickly.

a Describe the energy transfers that happen as the cyclist brakes. *2 marks*

The brake blocks on the wheels have a total mass of 0.10 kg and are made from a material with a specific heat capacity of 2.0 kJ/kg°C. During braking the temperature of the blocks increases by 5.0°C.

b   Calculate the increase in thermal energy of the brake blocks.   `3 marks`

....

....

17 A bungie jumper of mass 50 kg jumps from a bridge and bounces on the end of the cord several times. They eventually stop bouncing and finish 50 m below their starting point.

a   Calculate the change in gravitational potential energy of the jumper.   `2 marks`

....

....

The bungie cord used during this jump has a mass of 30 kg and a specific heat capacity 1.9 kJ/kg°C.

b   Assuming that all of the gravitational potential energy is transferred to the thermal store of the bungee cord evenly, calculate the change in temperature for the cord.   `2 marks`

....

....

18 A crane is used to lift a pallet of bricks of mass 400 kg through a distance of 30 m. This process takes one minute. (Use gravitational field strength = 9.8 N/kg.)

a   Calculate the change in potential energy of the bricks.   `2 marks`

....

....

b   Calculate the effective power of the crane during the lifting process.   `3 marks`

....

....

....

c   The electrical power rating of the motor doing the lifting is 2.5 kW. Calculate the efficiency of the motor during the lifting process.   `2 marks`

....

....

19 An elevator is powered by an electric motor with a power rating of 4.0 kW. The mass of the empty elevator is 600 kg. (Use gravitational field strength = 9.8 N/kg.)

a   How long would it take for the motor to lift the elevator through a height of 3.0 m?   `3 marks`

....

....

....

Questions marked **1** **1** are for Combined Science Trilogy and GCSE Physics students

b Explain why the elevator takes longer to travel through this height when it is full of passengers.

`2 marks`

....

....

Electricity

Current, potential difference and resistance

Standard circuit diagram symbols

Circuit symbols are used to show how components are connected in a circuit.

1 Match the component symbol to the name and then to the purpose of that component.

`14 marks`

Symbol		Component		Purpose
		Ammeter		A component that resists the current in a circuit depending on the temperature.
		Cell		A component that allows current to pass through it in one direction and also gives out light.
		Light-emitting diode		A component that resists a current in the circuit depending on the light level.
		Thermistor		A component that powers a circuit by providing a voltage.
		Light-dependent resistor		A component that allows current to pass through it in only one direction.
		Voltmeter		A component that measures the potential difference across another component.
		Diode		A device that measures the current in part of a circuit.

2 In the space here draw a circuit diagram showing a **battery** connected to a **lamp** through a **switch** and a **variable resistor**.

`4 marks`

Electrical charge and current

A electric current is a flow of charge caused by a potential difference acting on a circuit.

> total charge flow = current × time

Questions marked 1 1 are for GCSE Physics students only

3 Complete the following sentences using the words below. `5 marks`

coulomb   charge   current   amperes   time

The size of an electric .... is the rate of flow of ....

charge flow = current × ....

$$[Q = It]$$

Electric charge is measured in a unit called the .... Current is measured in

....

4 Complete the table – be careful with conversion of units. `4 marks`

Charge	Current	Time
	3.5 A	15 s
	20 mA	1 min
32 C		120 s
300 µC	0.75 mA	

Current, resistance and potential difference

The current in a circuit depends on the resistance and potential difference acting. This gives the relationship:

potential difference = current × resistance

5 The table below shows three circuits. Use the information from the circuit diagrams to complete the bottom row in the table. `5 marks`

Circuit A	Circuit B	Circuit C
Potential difference: .... Current: .... Resistance:	Potential difference: .... Current: .... Resistance:	Potential difference: .... Current: .... Resistance: ....

Required practical activity 3

A group of students investigated how the resistance of a wire varied with its length. Their results are shown in the table below.

Length (cm)	10.0	15.0	20.0	30.0	35.0	40.0
Current (A)	3.01	2.02	1.49	1.20	1.00	0.86
Potential difference (V)	6.00	6.00	6.00	6.01	6.00	6.02
Resistance (Ω)						

Questions marked **1** **1** are for Combined Science Trilogy and GCSE Physics students

6 Use the information to plot a graph comparing the length of the wire to its resistance.

5 marks

7 Use the graph to describe the relationship between the length of the wire and its resistance.

2 marks

Description:

....

....

Resistors

For some components the resistance is constant but for others it can change. Graphs showing current against potential difference can be used to describe any changes in resistance.

The graphs below show how the current in a component varies with the potential difference for three different components.

Wire at constant temperature	Lamp filament	Diode

8 Match the following six descriptions to the components by writing the correct letters in the boxes above. The statements can be used more than once.

8 marks

A	B	C
When the current is low the current is proportional to the potential difference.	The behaviour of the component is the same no matter what the direction of the current.	The resistance of the component increases when the current is high.
D	**E**	**F**
The resistance of the component is very high for very small potential differences.	The behaviour of the component depends on the direction of the potential difference acting across it.	The resistance of the component stays constant when the current is high.

Questions marked 🔵 🔴 are for GCSE Physics students only

9 Thermistors have a resistance that changes with temperature. A student wants to investigate how the resistance of a thermistor varies as the temperature falls. They connect the thermistor to a battery, ammeter and voltmeter.

Sketch a suitable circuit for measuring the current in the thermistor and the potential difference across it during the experiment.

3 marks

10 Number the following stages in the order they would need to be carried out during this thermistor experiment.

6 marks

Stage	
1	Pour some boiling water from a kettle into a beaker.
	Repeat from stage 5.
	Record the temperature, the current in the resistor and the potential difference across it.
	Place the thermistor into the beaker of water.
	Wait for 1 minute until the thermistor reaches the same temperature as the water.
	Connect the thermistor into the circuit.
	Allow the water to cool for three minutes.
8	
9	

11 Add the final two stages (8 and 9) to the thermistor experiment to produce a graph showing the relationship between the temperature of the thermistor and its resistance.

2 marks

12 Why is it safer to use a 1.5 V battery in this experiment instead of a mains-powered supply?

1 mark

Required practical activity 4 (resistance of a filament lamp)

A student has set up a circuit to investigate the current–voltage characteristics of a filament lamp. The circuit contains a power supply, filament lamp, variable resistor, ammeter and voltmeter.

Questions marked 1 1 are for Combined Science Trilogy and GCSE Physics students

13 Circle the mistakes in the circuit diagram. `5 marks`

14 Sketch the correct circuit alongside it. `4 marks`

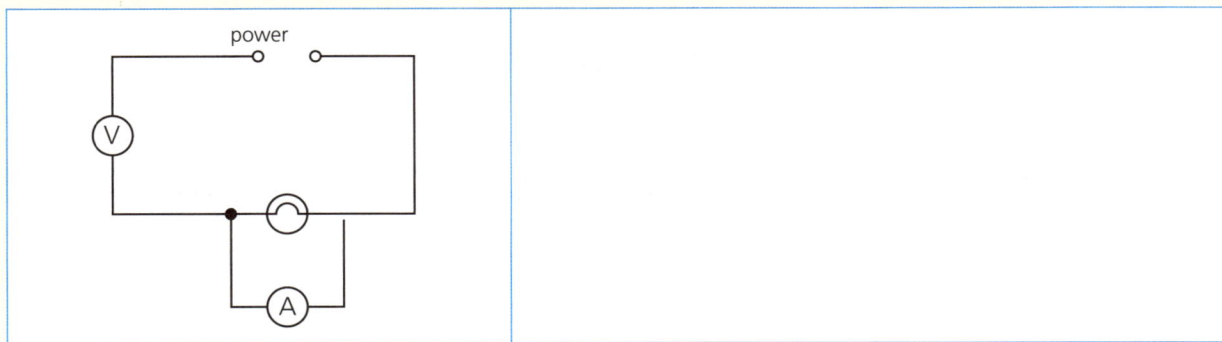

Series and parallel circuits

In a series section of a circuit the current is the same throughout and the potential difference of the power supply is shared between components. The total resistance is the sum of the resistances in series. In a parallel section of a circuit the potential difference is the same across all components and the total current is the sum of the currents in each branch. The resistance is lower than the resistance of the smallest resistance in any branch.

Components in circuits can be connected in series or in parallel.

15 Draw example circuits in the table below to show the difference between components connected in series and in parallel. `2 marks`

Three lamps in series	Three resistors in parallel

16 For each of the statements in the table below write whether the statements made are about a pair of components in series (**S**) or a pair of components in parallel (**P**). `6 marks`

Statement	S or P
The potential difference across the components is the same.	
The total current in the circuit is the sum of the current through the two components.	
The same current passes through each component.	

Statement	S or P
The total resistance is less than the resistance of the smallest resistor.	
The total potential difference of the power supply is the same as the sum of the potential differences of the two components.	
The total resistance is the sum of all the resistors.	

17 The circuit diagrams below show combinations of resistors. For each one circle the total resistance between points X and Y. `3 marks`

| 10 Ω | 30 Ω | 60 Ω | 90 Ω |

| 10 Ω | 30 Ω | 60 Ω | 90 Ω |

| 10 Ω | 30 Ω | 60 Ω | 90 Ω |

Questions marked ① ① are for GCSE Physics students only

Domestic uses and safety

Mains electricity in the United Kingdom is 230 V alternating current. Three wires are used to connect devices to the mains: the live wire, a neutral wire and an earth wire, which acts as a safety device.

Direct and alternating potential difference

18 Complete the following sentences using the words below. **5 marks**

potential difference   alternating   direct   60   50   110   230   current   frequency

Mains electricity is an .... supply. The United Kingdom has a mains supply

with a .... of .... Hz and a .... of

.... V.

19 Add the words 'direct' or 'alternating' current to show the difference between the two. **2 marks**

- .... current: The current travels only in one direction.

- .... current: The direction of the current changes rapidly.

Mains electricity

In the United Kingdom mains plugs are connected using three wires. These are shown in the diagram.

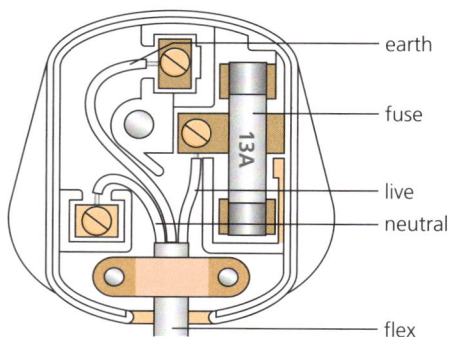

20 Colour (or label the colours) of the wires in this plug. **3 marks**

21 Add the following three labels to explain the functions of the wires. **6 marks**

  a Carries the alternating potential difference from the supply to the device.

  b Completes the circuit.

  c Acts as a safety wire to prevent the device becoming live.

22 Add the potential differences that the wires are at when they are operating correctly. **3 marks**

Energy transfers

Power

The power of an electrical device is given by:

power = potential difference × current

and power = (current)² × resistance

Questions marked 🔵 🟠 are for Combined Science Trilogy and GCSE Physics students

23 Use the two equations for electrical power to complete this table of information about some circuits. `8 marks`

Power	Potential difference	Current	Resistance
	6.0 V	2.0 A	
30 W	9.0 V		
	1.5 V	6.0 mA	
5.2 kW	230 V		

Energy transfers in everyday appliances

The energy transferred by a device can be calculated using:

energy = power × time

For an electrical device this can also be calculated using:

energy = charge flow × potential difference

24 The table shows some battery-powered electrical devices. Calculate their power ratings and fill in all the gaps. `4 marks`

Device	Mobile phone	Tablet	Laptop	Torch
Current (A)	1.4	2.3	4.00	
Potential difference (V)	8.0	12.0		3.0
Power (W)			48.0	1.5

25 Explain why a torch with a power rating of 2.0 W will last longer than a torch with a power rating of 5.0 W when powered by the same type of battery. `1 mark`

Explanation: ....

....

26 Fill in the gaps in this table about electrical energy. `4 marks`

Device	Potential difference	Current	Time used for	Energy transferred
Battery-powered torch	9.0 V	1.2 A	30 seconds	
Microwave oven	230 V	3.2 A	8 minutes	
Television	230 V		2 hours	3.73 MJ
Games console USA		3.5 A	3 hours	4.16 MJ

27 Use the information in the table above to suggest why microwave ovens are not battery powered. `1 mark`

Explanation: ....

....

28 An electric kettle in the UK operates with a potential difference of 230 V and a current of 4.5 V, while an electric kettle from the USA operates with a voltage of 110 V and a current of 5.0 A.

Work out the power ratings of these two devices and use that information to explain why it takes a lot longer to make a cup of tea in the USA. `1 mark`

Explanation: ....

....

The National Grid

The National Grid connects power stations to factories and homes. It uses step-up transformers to increase voltages to increase efficiency and step-down transformers to decrease voltages.

29 The diagram below shows a simplified picture of the National Grid. Draw lines from the labels to the correct parts of the diagram.

`8 marks`

	High ac voltage (25 000 V)	Very high ac voltage (250 000 V)	Low ac voltage (230 V)	
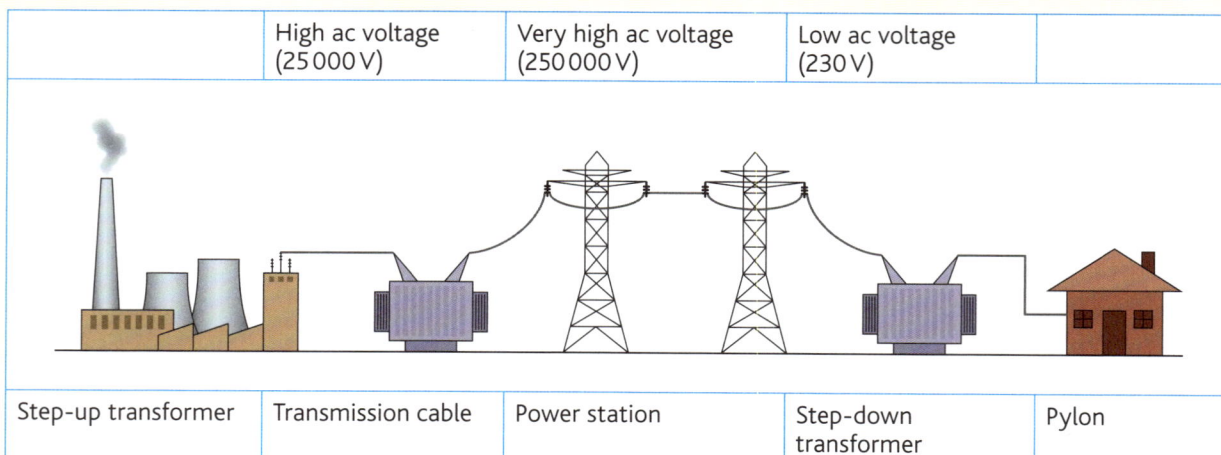				
Step-up transformer	Transmission cable	Power station	Step-down transformer	Pylon

30 The National Grid contains step-up transformers and step-down transformers. Complete these sentences explaining what the transformers are for.

`5 marks`

Step-up transformers .... the potential difference of an ac source such as

a power station. Transmitting electrical power at very .... voltages is very

efficient as it produces a .... heating effect in the wires due to the smaller

.... in them. Near to where the power is to be used step-down transformers

.... the ac potential difference so that the supply is safer to use.

Static electricity

Static charge

Charged objects have an electric field which surrounds them. This field affects other charged objects.

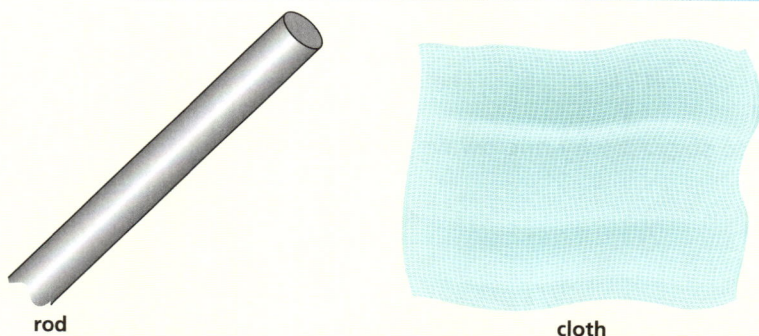

rod

cloth

This diagram shows a plastic rod that has become positively electrically charged when it was rubbed by a cloth.

31 Annotate the diagram to explain how the rod has become charged by describing the movement of any charged particles.

`2 marks`

32 Describe what will happen if the rod is placed close to another rod that has been rubbed using the same type of cloth.

`1 mark`

Electric fields

33 Complete the diagram to show the electric field pattern surrounding a proton. `2 marks`

Exam-style questions

34 The circuit below is used to investigate the relationship between the current in a diode and the potential difference across it.

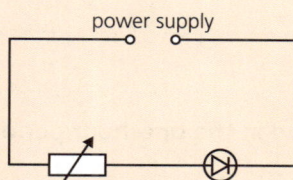

power supply

a Add an ammeter and a voltmeter to the diagram in the correct positions. `2 marks`

b Complete the results table by calculating the resistance of the diode when the potential difference is 1.00 V and 1.2 V. `2 marks`

Potential difference (V)	0.00	0.20	0.40	0.60	0.80	1.00	1.20
Current (mA)	0.00	0.01	0.02	0.20	2.50	11.30	3000
Resistance (Ω)	—	20 k	20 k	3.0 k	320		

c Describe how the results would be different if the direction of the potential difference were reversed. `2 marks`

35 A student connects a 3.0 V battery to a lamp in the simple circuit shown below. This causes a current of 1.5 A to flow in the lamp.

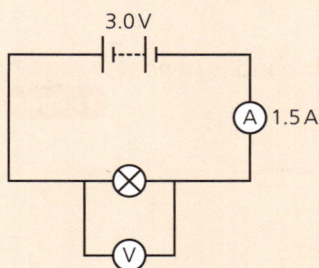

3.0 V

(A) 1.5 A

a What is the resistance of the lamp in the circuit? `2 marks`

....

....

b How much charge is transferred by the circuit if it operates for 5 minutes? `3 marks`

....

c The student replaces the 3.0 V battery with a 6.0 V battery and predicts that the new current will be 3.0 A. When measured the current in the lamp is 2.5 A.

Explain why the current in the lamp is not 3.0 A as the student expected. `3 marks`

....

....

....

Questions marked **1** **1** are for GCSE Physics students only

36 The circuit shown in the diagram below is powered by a 12.0 V battery.

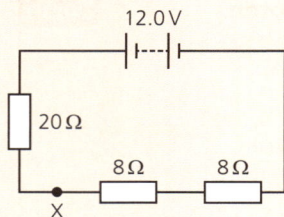

12.0 V

20 Ω

8 Ω   8 Ω

X

a Describe the type of circuit shown. `1 mark`

....

b Calculate the total resistance of the circuit. `1 mark`

....

c Calculate the current at point X in the circuit. `1 mark`

....

d Calculate the energy transferred by the circuit in one hour. `2 marks`

....

....

e How much charge is transferred in the one-hour period? `2 marks`

....

....

37 A mains-powered electrical heating element with a resistance of 66 Ω is used in a kettle.

a What is standard UK mains potential difference? `1 mark`

....

b What is the power of the kettle? `2 marks`

....

c How much energy is transferred by the kettle when it heats water for 2 minutes? `2 marks`

....

38 In an experiment a student notices that after walking on a carpet they experience a small electric shock when touching a metal door handle.

a Explain the cause of this spark and why it happened only when their hand is near the handle. `3 marks`

....

....

....

b Sketch the electric field pattern that surrounds a negatively charged sphere. `2 marks`

Particle model of matter

Density of materials

The particle arrangement in materials is related to their density, which is calculated using:

$$\text{density} = \frac{\text{mass}}{\text{volume}}$$

1 Sketch the particle arrangements in solids, liquid and gases. **3 marks**

Solids	Liquids	Gases

2 Explain how the diagrams you have drawn show these facts. **4 marks**

Fact	Explanation
a Solids have a much higher density compared with gases.	
b Gases and liquids are fluids, but solids are not.	

3 A group of students are measuring the densities of some solid metal cubes. Their measurements are shown in this table.

Length (m)	Width (m)	Height (m)	Volume (m³)	Mass (kg)	Density (kg/m³)
30.01×10^{-3}	30.05×10^{-3}	29.99×10^{-3}		0.218	

Complete the table. **2 marks**

4 The students use a micrometer to measure the length of the sides of the cube. Why is this instrument better than using a ruler? **1 mark**

....

5 Add these labels to this diagram to show the names for the different changes of state.

5 marks

melting   freezing   evaporating   condensing   subliming

solid

liquid

gas

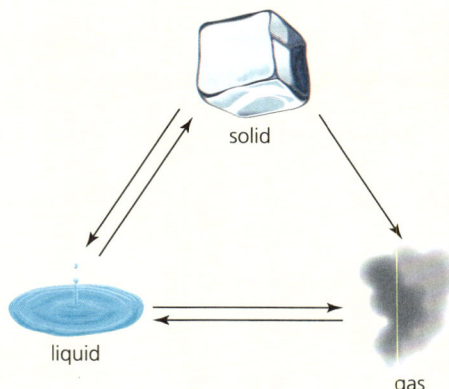

Internal energy and energy transfers

Energy is stored in a system when its temperature increases or it changes state. This energy is called 'internal energy'. When temperature changes then:

change in thermal energy = mass × specific heat capacity × temperature change

During a change of state:

energy change = mass × specific latent heat

6 Match the quantities and definitions by drawing lines.

3 marks

Quantity		Definition
Specific latent heat of fusion		The energy change when 1 kg of a material changes from a liquid to a gas due to heating
Specific heat capacity		The energy change when 1 kg of a material changes from a solid to a liquid
Specific latent heat of vaporisation		The energy change when 1 kg of a material increases its temperature by 1°C

7 Complete the following sentences using the words below.

6 marks

temperature   internal   state   particles   kinetic   potential

The energy stored by a system due to the .... that make up that

system is known as .... energy. This energy is the total of the

.... energy and .... energy of all of the particles.

Heating the system increases its internal energy and either increases the ....

or changes the .... (e.g. from solid to liquid).

8 Complete these two energy equations related to heating.   2 marks

change in thermal energy = mass × .... × temperature change

energy for a change of state = mass × ....

9 Complete this table using the relationship between changes in thermal energy, mass, specific heat capacity and temperature.   4 marks

Change in thermal energy	Mass (kg)	Specific heat capacity (J/kg °C)	Temperature change (°C)
	1.3	1200	15
400 J		120	4.0
30 kJ	0.50	4200	
2.50 kJ	1.40		2.0

10 Circle the correct answer to each of these three specific latent heat questions.   3 marks

a	b	c
How much energy is required to melt 0.20 kg of ice if the latent heat of fusion of ice is 334 kJ/°C?	What is the energy change when 2.0 grams of gold evaporates? The latent heat of vaporisation of gold is 63 kJ/°C.	What is the latent heat of fusion of mercury if there is an energy change of 3390 J when 0.3 kg of solid mercury melts?
66.8 kJ 668 kJ 0.69 kJ	126 kJ 126 J 31.5 J	113 J/kg 11.3 kJ/kg 1.02 J/kg

11 The graph below shows the temperature of a sample of water being heated.

Add the following labels to the graph.   5 marks

melting – no temperature change   vaporising – no temperature change

solid state   liquid state   gaseous state

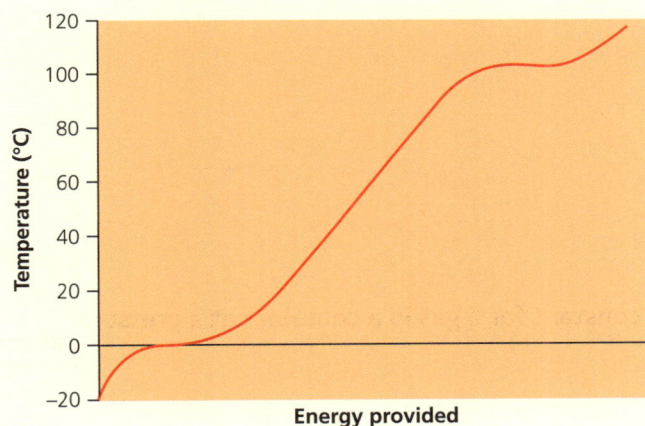

Particle model and pressure

Pressure in gases is caused by the moving particles colliding with the container walls. Pressure increases with temperature because the particles are moving faster. For a fixed mass of gas at constant temperature:

pressure × volume = constant

Compressing a gas can increase its temperature because work is being done on it.

12 Complete the following sentences, which explain how a gas causes pressure on a container.

7 marks

The particles in a gas are moving .... and in .... directions. When the particles .... with the container walls they produce a force.

When the gas is heated the .... energy of the particles increases and so does their average .... This .... the pressure on the container because there are .... energetic collisions between the particles and the walls.

13 The diagram below shows a small number of gas particles in a container with arrows representing their movement. Draw the same number of particles in the larger container and explain why increasing the volume of the container decreases the pressure.

2 marks

Explanation: ....
....
....

pressure × volume = constant

14 Use the relationship above to calculate the constant for a gas in a container at a pressure of 40 kPa and volume 0.25 m³.

1 mark

....

15 Use the constant from question **14** to work out the pressure of the gas sample when the volume is decreased to 0.15 m³.

1 mark

....

16 Which of the following can cause an increase in the internal energy of a gas?

2 marks

☐ doing mechanical work by compressing the gas quickly

☐ letting the gas expand rapidly

☐ cooling the gas

☐ heating the gas

Questions marked 🟦1 🟧1 are for Combined Science Trilogy and GCSE Physics students

Exam-style questions

17 A group of students investigated the melting of ice when heated by an electric heater. They put a measured mass of ice in a funnel and heated it for two minutes. After this time, they measured the mass of ice remaining and the energy supplied to the ice.

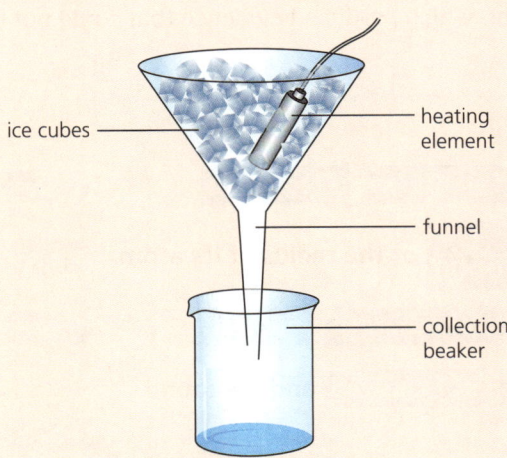

- Mass of ice before the experiment: 0.45 kg
- Mass of ice remaining at the end of the experiment: 0.33 kg
- Energy provided by the heater: 3600 J

ice cubes

heating element

funnel

collection beaker

a Calculate the latent heat of fusion of ice using the measurements the students made. **3 marks**

....

....

....

Their measurements are shown alongside the diagram.

b The value the students calculated for the latent heat of fusion was **lower** than the true value. Which of the following could be a cause for this lower answer? **1 mark**

☐ The heating element was faulty and did not heat the ice.
☐ Some of the ice melted due to heating from the room.
☐ The temperature of the ice was lower than 0°C at the start of the experiment.
☐ The temperature of the ice was higher than 0°C at the start of the experiment.

To check results, the students collected the water produced when the ice melted. The collected water had a volume of 119 cm³. The density of pure water at 0°C is 1000 kg m³.

c Calculate the mass of water collected. **3 marks**

....

....

....

18 A sample of gas is held in a container. The pressure caused by the gas is 40 kPa and the volume is 0.20 m³. The gas is compressed further by reducing the volume of the container to 0.15 m³ while the temperature is kept the same.

a Calculate the new pressure of the gas. **2 marks**

....

....

b Explain how and why the pressure would be different if the temperature of the gas had been allowed to rise as it was compressed. **3 marks**

....

....

....

Questions marked **1** **1** are for GCSE Physics students only

Atomic structure

The structure of the atom

Atoms have a very tiny radius and are composed of a nucleus, containing protons and neutrons, which is surrounded by electrons in energy levels. Atoms of a particular element have the same number of protons (same atomic number) but may have different numbers of neutrons if they are different isotopes. The nuclear model of the atom was discovered using an alpha particle scattering experiment, which produced evidence that could not be explained by the previous model.

1 Circle the correct option for each statement:

a Atoms have a radius of approximately 1×10^{-6} m | 1×10^{-10} m | 1×10^{-16} m . **1 mark**

b The radius of a nucleus is less than $\dfrac{1}{100}$ $\dfrac{1}{1000}$ $\dfrac{1}{10000}$ of the radius of its atom. **1 mark**

c The nucleus of an atom is positively charged | negatively charged | neutral . **1 mark**

d Protons are positively charged | negatively charged | not charged and are found inside | outside the nucleus. **2 marks**

e Electrons are positively charged | negatively charged | not charged and are found inside | outside the nucleus. **2 marks**

f Neutrons are positively charged | negatively charged | not charged and are found inside | outside the nucleus. **2 marks**

2 Atoms are often represented in the notation shown here:

$$^{27}_{13}\text{Al}$$

a Draw a circle round the atomic number in the symbol. **1 mark**

b Draw a box round the mass number in the symbol. **1 mark**

c Complete this sentence by filling in the blanks. **1 mark**

The atomic number of an atom is the number of .... in the nucleus.

The mass number of an atom is the number of protons plus .... in the nucleus.

d Explain how you work out the number of neutrons in the nucleus using the two numbers described above. **1 mark**

....

....

3 The boxes show a list of isotopes of oxygen, carbon and uranium.

Isotope	$^{16}_{8}\text{O}$	$^{12}_{6}\text{C}$	$^{238}_{92}\text{U}$	$^{13}_{8}\text{O}$	C	U
Number of protons					6	92
Number of neutrons					8	143
Number of electrons					6	92

a Complete the table to show the numbers of protons, neutrons and electrons in the atoms – don't forget the 'C' and the 'U' in the isotope row. **16 marks**

Questions marked **1** **1** are for Combined Science Trilogy and GCSE Physics students

b What do all isotopes of oxygen have in common?

....

....

4 The nuclear model of the atoms was first discovered through an alpha particle scattering experiment. The diagram below shows the start of the paths of some alpha particles as they pass near a nucleus.

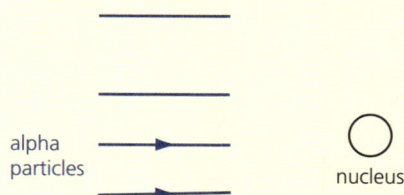

alpha
particles ⟶
      ⟶   ○
                nucleus

a Complete the paths and describe them using these labels: 4 marks

| no deflection | small deflection |

| large deflection | reflects back from the nucleus |

b Explain why the alpha particles passing closest to the nucleus are deflected most. 2 marks

....

....

Atoms and nuclear radiation

Unstable nuclei can decay by several methods including alpha decay, beta decay, gamma decay and neutron emission. These emissions have different properties and cause different changes to the nucleus. Decays can be shown using decay equations. Radioactive decay is random. The half-life of an isotope is the time it takes for the number of nuclei to fall to half.

5 Complete this sentence using the words below to explain why some materials are radioactive. 6 marks

| unstable | activity | random | becquerel | stable | radiation |

Radioactive decay is a .... process that happens to ....

nuclei. The nucleus gives out .... and becomes more ....

The rate at which the material decays is called its .... and is measured

in ....

6 This diagram shows some of the properties of alpha, beta and gamma radiation. Connect each radiation to the correct properties. One has been done for you. **13 marks**

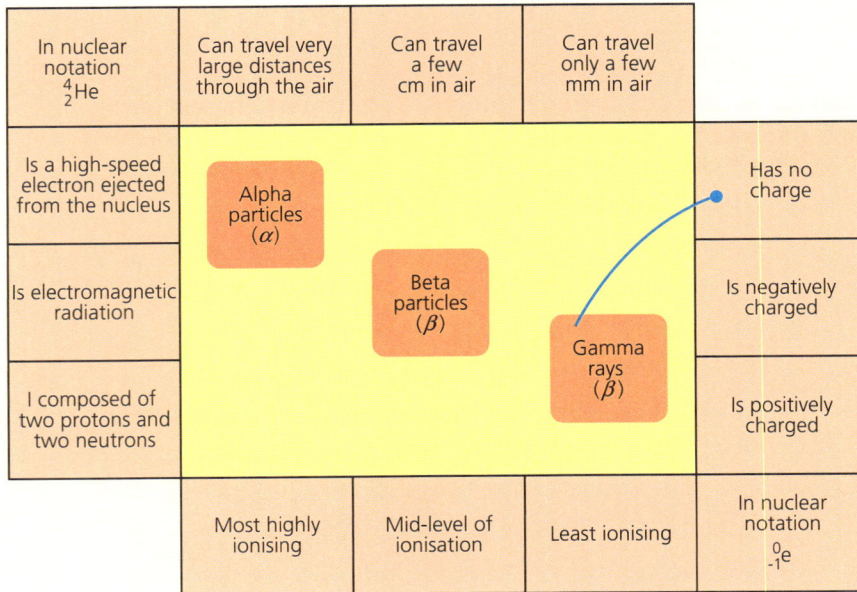

In nuclear notation ^4_2He	Can travel very large distances through the air	Can travel a few cm in air	Can travel only a few mm in air
Is a high-speed electron ejected from the nucleus	Alpha particles (α)		Has no charge
Is electromagnetic radiation	Beta particles (β)		Is negatively charged
I composed of two protons and two neutrons	Gamma rays (β)		Is positively charged
	Most highly ionising	Mid-level of ionisation	Least ionising	In nuclear notation $^0_{-1}e$

7 Complete the following set of equations showing nuclear decay by inserting the missing atomic numbers and mass numbers. **14 marks**

Alpha decays	Beta decays
$^{222}_{88}Ra \rightarrow ^{218}_{86}Rn + \text{......................}$	$^{14}_{6}C \rightarrow ^{14}_{7}N + \text{......................}$
$^{185}_{79}Au \rightarrow \square_\square Ir + ^4_2He$	$^8_3Li \rightarrow \square_\square Be + ^0_{-1}e$
$\square_{84}Po \rightarrow ^{204}Pb + ^4_2He$	$^{201}_\square Au \rightarrow ^\square_{80}Hg + ^0_{-1}e$

8 This graph shows the activity of a sample of radioactive material over time.

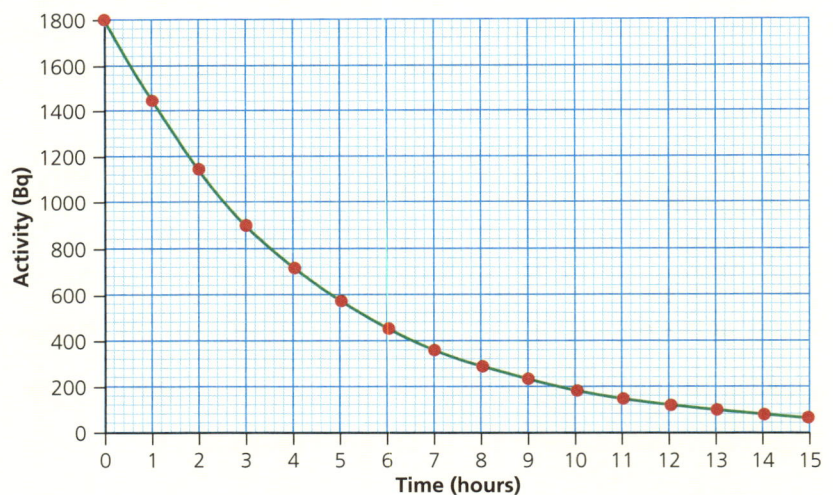

a Use the graph to find the half-life of the sample. Indicate this on the graph. **1 mark**

b If the half-life of a radioactive material is 3 years, what fraction of it will remain after:

   i 6 years .... **1 mark**

   ii 12 years .... **1 mark**

Questions marked **1** **1** are for Combined Science Trilogy and GCSE Physics students

Hazards and uses of radioactive emissions and of background radiation

There is a varying level of background radiation caused by natural and man-made sources.

9 The table shows some of the sources of radiation and the dose received from that source by one person in the United Kingdom during a year.

a Add an 'N' for natural sources and 'MM' for man-made sources to the second column in the table. **6 marks**

b Use the data to draw a pie chart representing the sources of the radiation dose. You can colour in the source column to act as a key. **6 marks**

Source	Natural or man-made	Dose in millisieverts (mSv)	Pie chart
Rocks		1.0	
Cosmic rays		0.25	
Medical treatment		10	
Nuclear fallout from weapons testing		0.01	
Exposure from eating food		5.0	
Nuclear fallout from power station accidents		0.01	

10 Radioactive sources have a very wide range of half-lives as shown in the table below.

a Rank the half-lives from longest (1) to shortest (5). **5 marks**

Isotope	Plutonium-241	Uranium-238	Carbon-12	Oxygen-13	Lithium-12
Half-life	14 years	4.5×10^8 years	5730 years	86×10^{-3} s	12×10^{-9} s
Rank					

b Which of the following has the longest half-life: **1 mark**

sodium-22 with a half-life of 2.60 years or cobalt-60 with a half-life of 166×10^6 seconds?

11 A radioactive tracer is used to detect organs that are not functioning correctly.

Tick (✓) the boxes showing properties that the tracer should have. **3 marks**

a half-life of less than a second	non-toxic	a half-life of over a year	emits only alpha particles
toxic	a half-life of several hours	emits only gamma rays	spreads out evenly throughout the body

Nuclear fission and fusion

Large nuclei can split in a process called fusion – this releases energy. Small nuclei can be fused together in stars and this also releases energy.

12 Complete these sentences describing nuclear fission using some of the words below. **6 marks**

gamma   neutron   unstable   joining   kinetic

elastic   splitting   small   smaller

Nuclear fission is the .... of an .... nucleus, which is

usually caused by the absorption of a .... The nucleus splits into two

.... nuclei releasing some neutrons and .... rays. The particles

released have .... energy and heat the surroundings when they are absorbed.

13 The diagram below shows the first stages of a fission chain reaction. Complete it and add some sentences to explain what is happening. **3 marks**

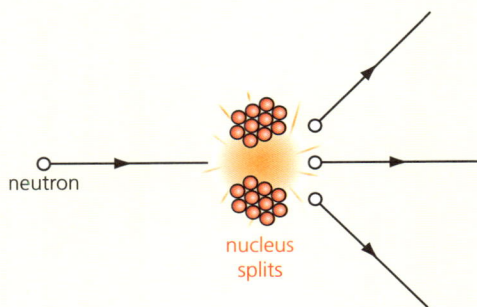

neutron

nucleus splits

....

....

14 In a typical fission chain reaction, the fission of one nucleus releases neutrons, which goes on to cause three further fissions, each of which releases three more neutrons and so on.

Stage	1	2	3	4	5	6	7	8
Fissions	1	3						

a Complete the table to show the number of fission reactions happening at each stage. **2 marks**

b Use the pattern to explain why the chain reaction will rapidly release very large amounts of energy. **1 mark**

....

....

15 Complete this sentence describing nuclear fusion by selecting the correct options. **5 marks**

Nuclear fusion is the breaking joining of two large small nuclei to form a larger smaller

nucleus. During this process some of the mass charge is converted into radiation charge .

Exam-style questions

16 In an investigation into the properties of two different radioactive materials a scientist measures the count rate for equal masses of the samples over a period of time. The graph showing this rate is given below.

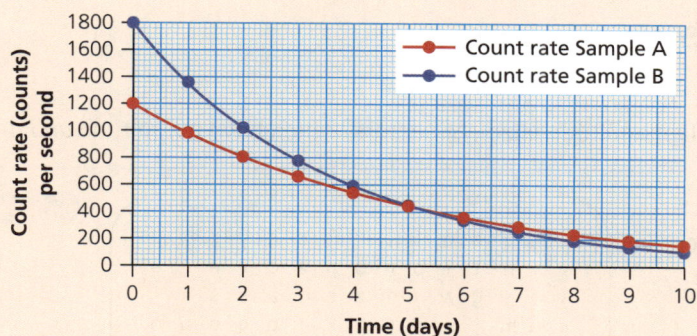

a Which of the materials has the longest half-life? `1 mark`

....

b What is the half-life of sample B? `1 mark`

....

17 The scientist then tests the penetrating power of the radiations to determine which type of radiation is being emitted by the samples by placing barriers between the samples and the detector. The results are shown in the table below.

Sample	Count rate after the barrier		
	no barrier	thin paper barrier	aluminium barrier
A	60	58	2
B	40	0	0

a What types of radiation are being emitted by the samples? `2 marks`

Sample A ....

Sample B ....

A sample of a different radioactive isotope (strontium-90) decays by beta particle emission.

b Complete the following decay equation. `3 marks`

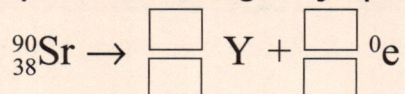

$$^{90}_{38}\text{Sr} \rightarrow \boxed{}\ \text{Y} + \boxed{}\ ^{0}\text{e}$$

c There are several isotopes of strontium. What property do all isotopes of strontium have in common? `1 mark`

....

Paper 2

Forces

Forces and their interactions

Scalar and vector quantities

Quantities can be either scalars, which have only magnitude (size), or vectors, which have magnitude *and* direction.

1 This word search contains nine words related to forces and movement. These hidden words match the clues in the table below. Complete the definitions then find the words in the word search. State the units that the quantity is measured in and then decide whether the quantity is a vector (V) or a scalar (S).

9 marks

```
e t q d o f i k m u d y x k v
v y h t i p n o p e q v n u e
s t j g w s m z e m a s s x l
k p m j i e p p k l p e n u o
s u h x n e s l n f x x h w c
y y b t h a w w a v n b x e i
n c u k r w g q m c p d c c t
t m e c n a t s i d e u q r y
i y v f d k a x g u d m y o c
a c c e l e r a t i o n e f l
q g b h l i o q x n v u y n f
p f p p i m s q i i v z p s t
i p k o d g n l e k m n k m d
y b e q f a z i d q h d q o l
f f a b q u q y d c v i j m u
```

Clue	Key word	Unit	V or S
The rate at which the velocity of something is changing			
The amount of matter in an object			
The force acting on an object due to gravity			
The speed of an object in a particular direction			
The cause of change of velocity			
The rate of change of distance			
The product of the mass and velocity of an object			
How far something has travelled overall, regardless of direction			
The distance in a particular direction measured from a starting point			

Contact and non-contact forces

Contact forces operate when objects touch, but non-contact forces operate whether the objects are touching or not.

Gravity	Upthrust	Electrostatic
Friction	Normal contact force	Air resistance
Drag	Electromagnetic	Tension

2 For the forces listed in the table above. Shade the contact forces in one colour and the non-contact forces in another. Provide a key.

3 marks

Questions marked **1** **1** are for Combined Science Trilogy and GCSE Physics students

Gravity

The weight of an object is caused by gravity. The Earth has a gravitational field that surrounds it, which has strength of 9.8 N/kg. To calculate the weight of an object use the relationship:

weight = mass × gravitational field strength

The 'centre of mass' is the point at which an object's weight seems to act.

3 Complete the table using the relationship between the weight, mass and gravitational field strength.

3 marks

Weight (N)	Mass (kg)	Gravitational field strength (N/kg)
	12.0	9.8
1960		9.8
220	55	

Resultant forces

The forces acting on an object can be added together, taking into account their direction, to find the resultant force that has the same overall effect. Free body diagrams can be used to represent the forces acting on objects and these vector diagrams can be used to find the resultant force by scale drawing. Single forces can also be broken down into two perpendicular components, which have the same effect as the original force.

4 The three diagrams show three objects with forces acting on them.

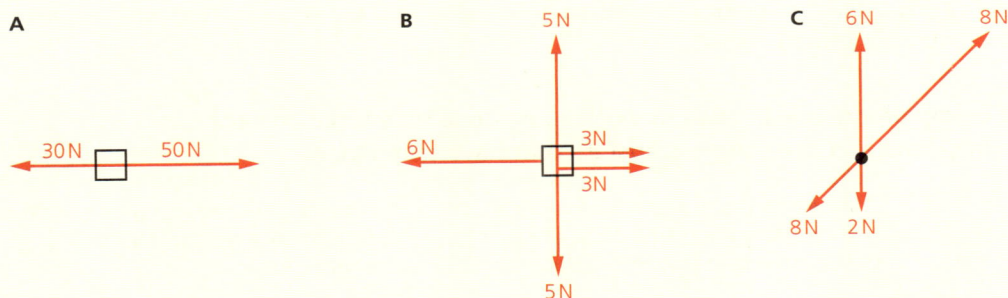

A

30N ← □ → 50N

B

5N ↑
6N ← □ → 3N
3N →
↓ 5N

C

6N ↑   ↗ 8N
●
↙ 8N   2N

a Draw the resultant force for each of these three simple scenarios. **3 marks**

b Which object is in equilibrium? .... **1 mark**

5 The diagram below shows a ball on a slope. The normal contact force acting on the ball is shown in red.

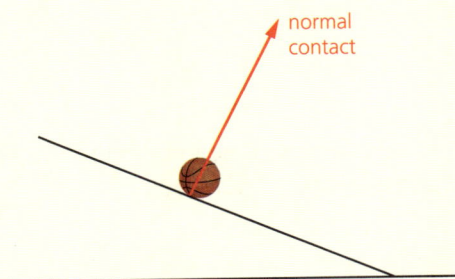

normal contact

a Resolve the force into two perpendicular components – vertical and horizontal. Draw these on the diagram. **2 marks**

Questions marked **1** **1** are for GCSE Physics students only

b Use the idea of a 'horizontal component' to explain why the ball rolls down the slope. `1 mark`

....

....

6 A boat has a force of 4000 N pushing it northwards across a river, but the flow of the river produces a force of 3000 N pushing it to the east.

a Use the space to the right to draw a scale diagram to find the magnitude of the resultant of these two forces. `2 marks`

Magnitude = ...

b Use a protractor to measure the angle that the force acts. .... `1 mark`

Work done and energy transfer

A force causing an object to move through a distance does work. The work done is calculated using:

work done = force × distance (moved in direction of the force)

Doing work is a transfer of energy and so work is measured in joules, which are equivalent to newton-meters. Working against friction causes a heating effect.

7 The two boxes below describe examples of work being done by a force. In each case calculate the work done and the energy transfers that have taken place. `8 marks`

	A person drags a box 3.0 m across the floor using a force of 25 N. The box is not moving at the end of the process.	A battery-powered motor lifts a set of masses with a weight 0.55 N through a distance of 60 cm.
How much work is done?		
What energy transfers have taken place?		

Forces and elasticity

Forces can cause a change in the shape of an object; these changes may reverse when the force is removed (elastic distortion) or may cause a permanent change (plastic deformation). When a spring is stretched:

force = spring constant × extension

so long as the spring is not stretched beyond its limit of proportionality. When a material is stretched the energy stored can be calculated using:

$$E_e = \frac{1}{2} k\, e^2$$

Questions marked **1** **1** are for Combined Science Trilogy and GCSE Physics students

8 This diagram shows such a graph plotted for a spring carrying different weights.

a Use the graph to find the spring constant for the spring being tested.

`2 marks`

b How much energy is stored in the spring when there is a force of 6.0 N acting on it?

`2 marks`

c Explain the behaviour of the spring when a force greater than 7 N acts on it.

`1 mark`

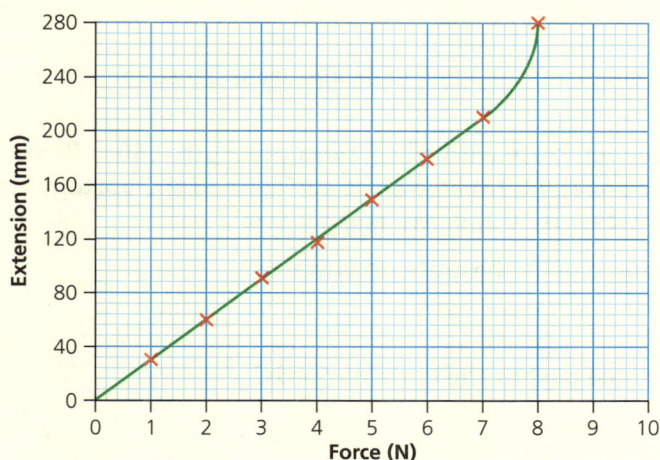

Moments, levers and gears

Forces can cause objects to rotate. The turning effect of a force is called a 'moment', found using:

moment = force × distance

If the anticlockwise moment and the clockwise moment are equal, then the object is balanced. A lever uses the principle of moments to increase the size of forces acting on objects, and gears can be used to transmit the rotational effect of forces.

9 A lever is used to attempt to lift a rock as shown in the diagram. If the rock has a weight of 600 N how large a force pushing down will be needed to lift the rock?

`1 mark`

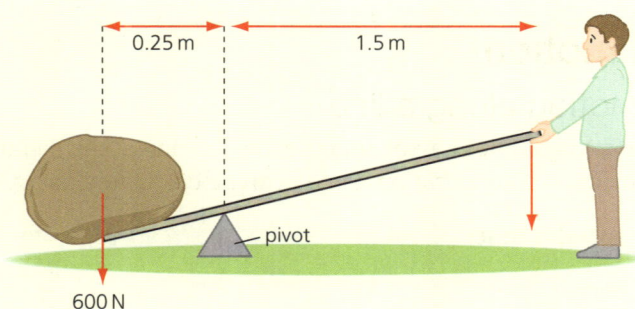

10 The diagram on the right shows four sacks and a swing balance with three hooks.

a Draw the sacks on the balance so that it is in equilibrium. You can put more than one sack on each hook.

`1 mark`

b Explain why the swing balance is in equilibrium.

`2 marks`

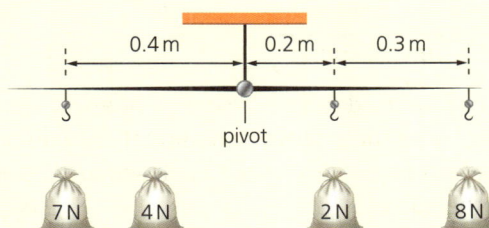

Pressure and pressure differences

Pressure in a fluid (1 and 2)

Liquids and gases are fluids and the pressures within them causes forces normal to the surfaces of containers they are inside. This pressure is calculated using:

$$p = \frac{F}{A}$$

Questions marked 1 1 are for GCSE Physics students only

The pressure at the bottom of a column of liquid is calculated using:

$$p = h \rho g$$

and the pressure differences at different depths cause a resultant force on submerged objects called the 'upthrust'.

---

11 A cubic wooden crate with all six sides of length 0.50 m floats in a pool of water so that the top face of the box is 1.00 m below the surface and the bottom face is 1.50 m below the surface. The density of water is 1000 kg/m³ and g = 9.8.

   a What force pulls the crate downwards? `1 mark`

   b What force pushes the crate upwards? `1 mark`

   c What is the size of the force acting on the top surface of the crate? `2 marks`

   d What is the size of the force acting on the bottom surface of the crate? `2 marks`

   e What is the weight of the crate? `1 mark`

Force and motion

Describing motion along a line

Objects moving in straight lines can be analysed by looking at the distance they travel, their speed and also their displacement, velocity and acceleration. Speed can be calculated using:

$$\text{distance} = \text{speed} \times \text{time}$$

and acceleration from:

$$\text{acceleration} = \frac{\text{change in velocity}}{\text{time taken}}$$

Distance–time graphs can be used to show movement and speed can be worked out using their gradients. Velocity–time graphs can also show movement, and these can be used to work out the acceleration from the gradient, and the distance travelled from their enclosed area. Objects that experience uniform acceleration can be analysed using the equation:

$$v^2 - u^2 = 2 a s$$

while an object falling through a fluid will show varying acceleration depending on the changing resultant force acting on it.

---

12 The table show some typical speeds. Connect the activities to the correct approximate value for the speeds. `5 marks`

cycling	walking	car on motorway	running	sound (in air)

~ 1.5 m/s	~ 6 m/s	~ 3 m/s	~ 330 m/s	~ 30 m/s

Questions marked 1 1 are for Combined Science Trilogy and GCSE Physics students

13 The graph on the right is a distance–time graph for a lift moving up a building.

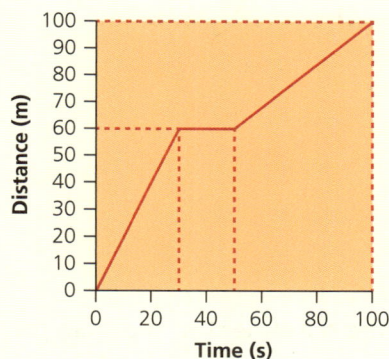

  a Describe the movement of the lift.

  3 marks

  ....

  ....

  ....

  b Use the graph to work out the top speed of the lift.

  1 mark

  ....

14 An asteroid orbits the Sun in a circular orbit at a constant distance. The period of the orbit is 900 days and the distance it travels is 20×10^{12} m.

  a Calculate the average speed of the asteroid in m/s.

  2 marks

  ....

  ....

  b Describe any changes in the speed and velocity of the asteroid during the orbit.

  2 marks

  ....

  ....

15 This graph shows the movement of a ball that starts off rolling down a slope.

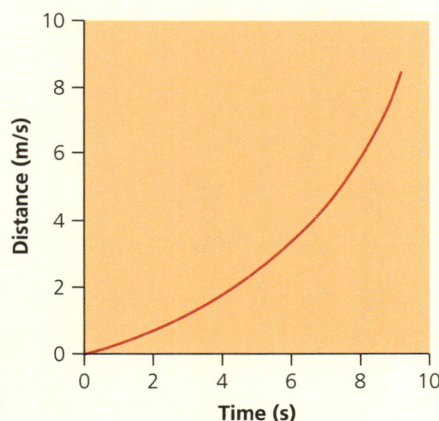

  a Describe how the graph shows that the speed of the ball is changing.

  1 mark

  ....

  ....

  b Draw a tangent to the line at time = 6 s and use this to work out the speed of the ball at that time.

  2 marks

  ....

  ....

16 A motorcycle takes 4.0 seconds to accelerate from 6.0 m/s to 15 m/s. What is the acceleration of the motorcycle?

  1 mark

  ....

17 This graph shows a velocity–time graph for a tram moving between two stops.

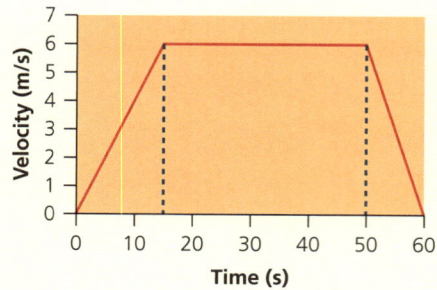

a Describe the movement of the tram for:

   i the first 15 seconds .... `1 mark`

   ii the next 35 seconds .... `1 mark`

   iii the last 10 seconds. .... `1 mark`

b Calculate the acceleration of the tram during the first 15 seconds. `1 mark`

....

c Work out the total distance travelled by the tram during the minute journey. `1 mark`

....

18 Complete the following table using the relationship: `3 marks`

$$(\text{final velocity})^2 - (\text{initial velocity})^2 = 2 \times \text{acceleration} \times \text{distance}$$

Final velocity (m/s)	Initial velocity (m/s)	Acceleration (m/s²)	Distance travelled (m)
36	0	8	
8	2		200
	0	9.8	4.5

19 The graph below shows how the velocity of a skydiver with a weight of 750 N changes after jumping from a plane.

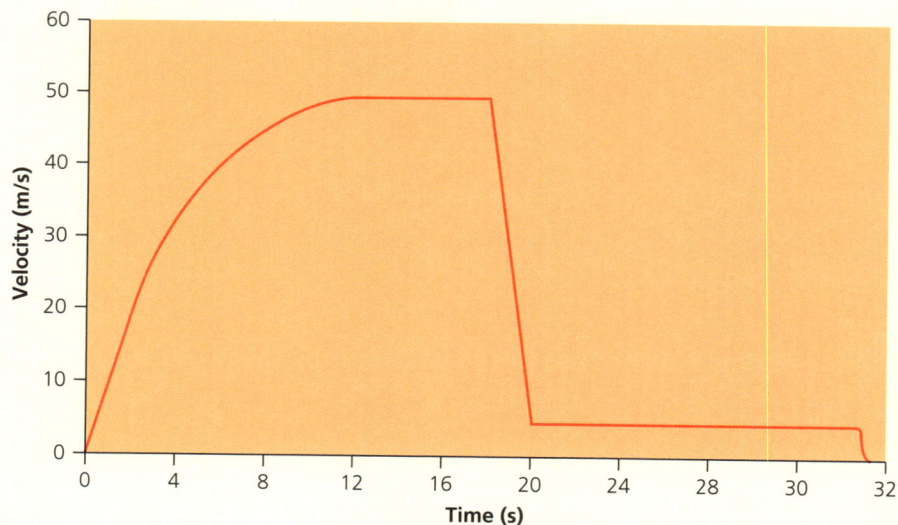

a Add the following labels to the diagram. `6 marks`

   ■ parachute opens
   ■ terminal velocity
   ■ large acceleration

Questions marked **1** **1** are for Combined Science Trilogy and GCSE Physics students

- rapid deceleration
- parachutist hits the ground

b Estimate the acceleration when the diver opens the parachute. `1 mark`

c Use the following boxes to show the forces acting at different points in the motion and explain the changes in motion for the skydiver. `6 marks`

Stage	Immediately after jumping out of plane	Several seconds after jumping out of plane	At terminal velocity
Free body diagram			
Explanation			

Forces, accelerations and Newton's laws of motion

Newtons laws of motion describe the relationships between forces and the movement of objects. The relationship between force, mass and acceleration is:

force = mass × acceleration

When there is no resultant force there is no acceleration and the object is in equilibrium.

20 Use the words below to complete the sentences to describe the three laws of motion. `8 marks`

opposite   same   force   inversely proportional   proportional

stationary   moving   direction   equal

First law: If the resultant .... acting on an object is zero and:

- the object is stationary, it remains ....

- the object is moving, it continues to move at the same .... and in the same

.... So the object continues to move at the same velocity.

Second law: The acceleration of an object is .... to the resultant force acting on

the object, and .... to the mass of the object.

Third law: Whenever two objects interact, the forces they exert on each other are

.... and ....

21 A student is investigating how the mass of an object affects its acceleration.

a What does the symbol '∝' mean? `1 mark`

....

....

b Which of these equations shows the expected relationship in this investigation?

Circle the correct one. `1 mark`

$a \propto F$ $a \propto m$ $a \propto \dfrac{1}{m}$ $a \propto 2m$ $a \propto \dfrac{1}{F}$

c What are the variables in this experiment? Complete the table. `3 marks`

Independent variable	
Dependent variable	
Control variables	

d The results of the experiment are shown in the table. Add a row showing 1/mass. `2 marks`

Mass (kg)	1.0	1.5	2.0	2.5	3.0	3.5
Acceleration in (m/s$_2$)	4.00	2.67	2.00	1.60	1.33	1.14
1/m (kg^{-1})						

e Use the graph paper to show a **linear** relationship between the variables. `3 marks`

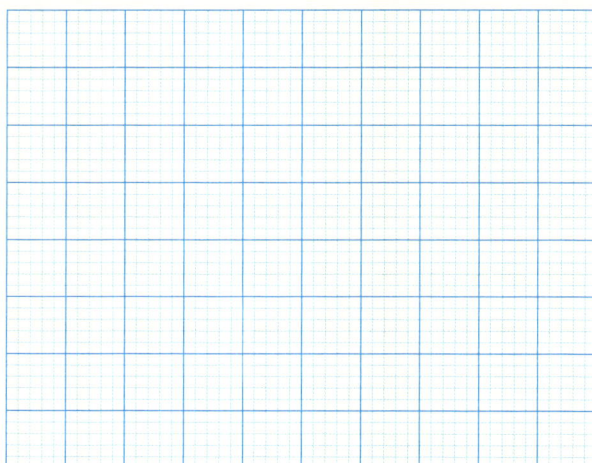

f What is the relationship? `1 mark`

g Use the graph to work out the size of the accelerating force. `2 marks`

Forces and braking

The stopping distance of a car is the sum of the thinking distance and the braking distance. Thinking distance depends on a person's reaction time, which is affected by a wide range of factors such as speed, concentration and alcohol consumption. Braking distance also depends on many factors including speed, road and brake conditions and the mass of the vehicle.

22 Estimate your reaction time. `1 mark`

23 How do these factors affect stopping distance? Write TD for factors which affect thinking distance, BD for braking distance or T&B for factors which affect both. `6 marks`

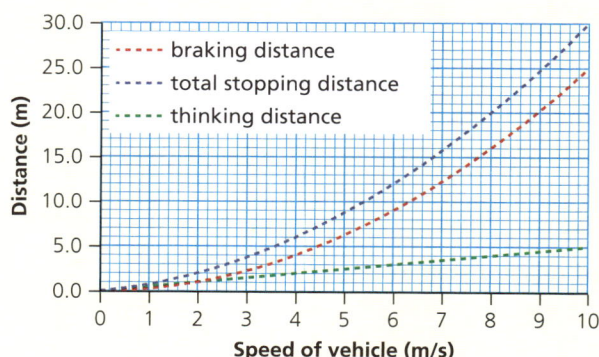

Distance (m) vs Speed of vehicle (m/s) graph showing braking distance, total stopping distance, thinking distance.

Condition of tyres	....
Tiredness	....
Wet road	....
Speed of vehicle	....
Alcohol consumption	....
Damaged brake disks	....

Questions marked 🔵 🟠 are for Combined Science Trilogy and GCSE Physics students

24 The graph on the previous page shows the thinking distance of the driver and the braking distance for a vehicle.

    a   Describe the relationship between the speed of a vehicle and the thinking distance. **1 mark**

....

    b   Describe the relationship between the speed and the braking distance. **1 mark**

....

    c   Use the graph to work out the overall stopping distance at 8 m/s. **1 mark**

....

25 The mass of a vehicle has a major effect on its stopping distance. For example a loaded lorry travelling at 20 m/s will have a longer stopping distance than a small car.

Explain this in terms of energy and the forces causing a vehicle to stop. **2 marks**

....

....

....

....

Momentum

Momentum is a property of a moving object given by:

momentum = mass × velocity

The principal of conservation of momentum says that, in a closed system, the momentum is always conserved. Forces cause changes in momentum according to:

$$F = \frac{m\Delta v}{\Delta t}$$

The concept of momentum can be used to explain how safety features of cars operate to reduce forces during collisions.

Momentum as a property of moving objects

26 Calculate the total momentum of each of these systems. Remember to take the direction of motion into account, with momentum to the right as positive and to the left as negative. **3 marks**

a	b	c
3.0 m/s → 4.0 kg	6 m/s → ← 2 m/s 2 kg 1 kg	4 m/s → ← 12 m/s 6 kg 2 kg
Momentum:.........................	Momentum:.........................	Momentum:.........................

Conservation of momentum

27 The top figure shows ball A closing in on ball B. The bottom figure shows the balls after they have collided and separated.

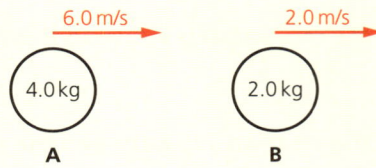

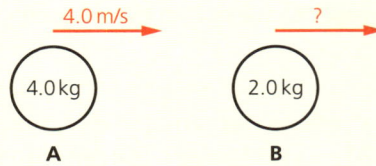

6.0 m/s →   2.0 m/s →

4.0 kg (A)   2.0 kg (B)

4.0 m/s →   ? →

4.0 kg (A)   2.0 kg (B)

a Calculate the total momentum of the balls before the collision. `1 mark`

b What is the total momentum after the collision? `1 mark`

c What is the momentum of ball A after the collision? `1 mark`

d Work out the velocity of ball B after the collision. `1 mark`

Changes in momentum

28 In a collision, an airbag slows down a head of mass 6.0 kg from 8 m/s to 0 m/s in a time of 0.5 s.

a Calculate the change in momentum of the head during the collision. `1 mark`

b Calculate the average force acting on the head during the collision. `1 mark`

c Explain how the airbag reduces the risk of head injury. `1 mark`

Questions marked **1** **1** are for Combined Science Trilogy and GCSE Physics students

Exam-style questions

29 A student investigated the extension of a spring by adding masses to the spring and measuring the extension as shown in the diagram. The results of this experiment are shown in the table below.

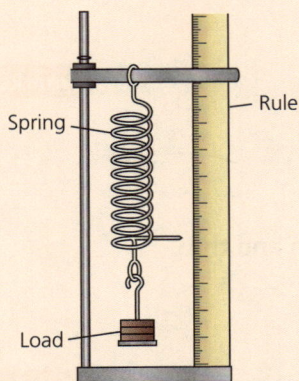

Spring — Rule

Load

Force (N)	0.00	1.00	2.00	3.00	4.00	5.00	6.00
Extension (m)	0	0.031	0.061	0.089	0.118	0.153	1.810

a What was the resolution of the ruler used in this experiment? **1 mark**

....

b Plot a graph showing the relationship between the force and the extension of the spring. **4 marks**

c Explain how this graph shows that the spring has stretched elastically during the experiment. `2 marks`

....

....

d Calculate the gradient of the graph. `2 marks`

....

....

e The relationship between the force acting on a spring, the extension and the spring constant is:

force = spring constant × extension

Use the gradient of the graph to calculate the spring constant for this spring. `2 marks`

....

....

f The energy stored by a stretched spring is given by:

elastic potential energy = 0.5 × spring constant × (extension)^2

....

A different spring has a spring constant of 450 N/m. Calculate the energy stored elastically by this spring when it is stretched by 40 cm. `2 marks`

....

30 An aeroplane of mass 3000 kg is accelerated by a constant resultant force of 9000 N.

a What is the acceleration of the aeroplane caused by this force? `3 marks`

....

....

....

....

b (final velocity)^2 − (initial velocity)^2 = 2 × acceleration × distance

What distance will the aeroplane travel if it is accelerated from rest to a take-off velocity of 60 m/s? `1 mark`

....

31 A car with mass 1500 kg is travelling at a constant speed of 25 m/s along a flat road as shown in the diagram.

a Which of the following statements are true?
Tick (✓) all that apply. `2 marks`

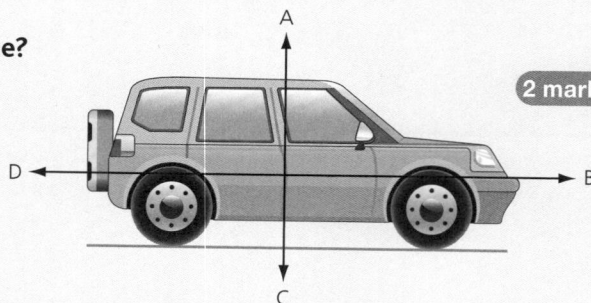

☐ Force A is equal in size to force B.

☐ Force A is equal in size to force C.

☐ Force B is equal in size to force D.

☐ Force B is greater than force D.

The driver sees a hazard and tries to stop the car. The driver's reaction time is 0.6 s.

Questions marked ❶ ❶ are for Combined Science Trilogy and GCSE Physics students

b Calculate the distance the car travels before the brakes are applied. `1 mark`

....

....

c Once braking begins the car comes to stop after an additional 50 m.
Calculate the deceleration of the car as it brakes. `2 marks`

....

....

d Calculate the average braking force causing the deceleration. `2 marks`

....

....

32 During a game of curling, a stone of mass 19 kg slides along the ice with a velocity of 0.50 m/s.

a Calculate the momentum of this stone. `1 mark`

....

....

b The first stone hits a second, stationary, stone with mass of 18 kg in a head-on collision. This second stone moves off with a velocity of 0.30 m/s.
Find the velocity of the first stone after the collision. `3 marks`

....

....

....

c The collision between the stones lasts for 0.10 seconds.
Calculate the average force during the impact. `2 marks`

....

....

....

Waves

Waves in air, fluids and solids

Transverse and longitudinal waves

There are two types of waves — longitudinal and transverse — which transfer energy without transferring material from place to place. Transverse waves have vibrations at right angles to the direction they travel (e.g. ripples on water) while longitudinal waves have particles that vibrate in the same direction as the wave travels.

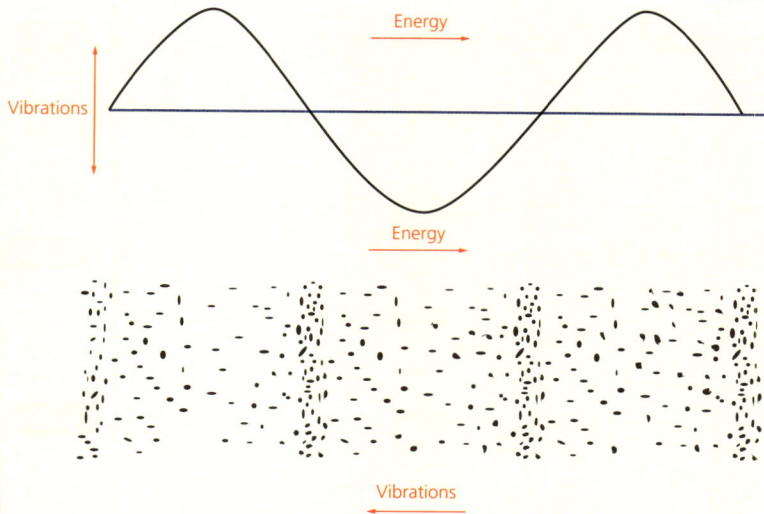

Energy

Vibrations

Energy

Vibrations

1 The diagram shows a representation of a transverse wave and a longitudinal wave. Mark on the diagram:

a the direction of energy transfer by each of the waves `2 marks`

b the direction of the vibrations `2 marks`

Properties of waves

Waves are described in terms of amplitude, wavelength, frequency and period. The speed of the wave is given by:

speed = frequency × wavelength

and the period of a wave is given by:

$$\text{period} = \frac{1}{\text{frequency}}$$

2 Complete this table to match the letters shown in the waves in the diagram above to the wave feature. You can use each letter more than once or not at all. `7 marks`

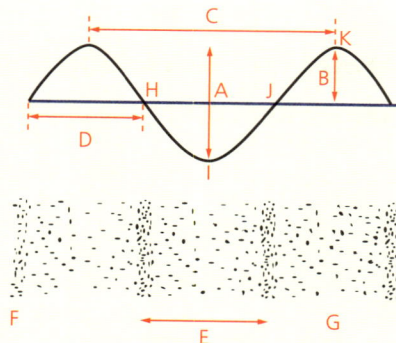

Wave feature	Wavelength	Amplitude	Crest	Trough	Compression	Rarefaction
Letter(s)						

3 Complete the table – be careful with conversion of units. `6 marks`

Wave speed	Wavelength	Frequency	Period
	0.20 m	400 Hz	
3.00×10^8 s		1.50 kHz	
	1.50×10^8 Hz		3.00×10^{-9} s

Reflection of waves

Waves can be reflected, absorbed or transmitted at the boundary between two materials. The angle of reflection for a reflected ray is equal to the angle of incidence for that ray. Absorption of waves causes heating of a material.

Questions marked 1 1 are for Combined Science Trilogy and GCSE Physics students

4 The diagram shows rays of light reaching the boundary between air and glass.

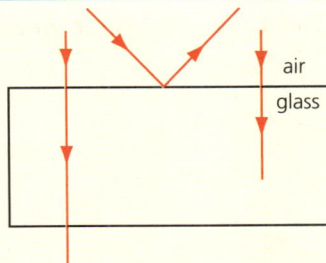

air

glass

a Label the arrows to show an incident, a reflected, an absorbed and a transmitted ray. `3 marks`

b Add a normal for the reflected ray. `1 mark`

c Mark two angles that are equal. `1 mark`

Sound waves

Sound waves are longitudinal waves that travel though gases as regions of compression and rarefaction. Sound waves in solids cause vibrations of the particles around their fixed positions. Our ears detect sound waves when the ear drum is vibrated by them – the vibrations are passed to the inner ear. This works for a limited range of frequencies.

5 Put the following sentences in order to give a description about how we hear sounds. `5 marks`

Order	Statement
	Sound waves travel through the air as a longitudinal wave.
	Vibrations in the ear drum are passed to the inner ear.
	A source of sound waves vibrates.
	Sound waves are absorbed by the ear drum and cause it to vibrate.
	Nerves in the inner ear detect vibrations and send electrical signals to the brain.

Waves for detection and exploration

Different waves can be used to make a range of observations. Ultrasonic waves can detect internal structures in objects or tissue layers in humans by analysing their echoes; seismic waves can show the internal structure of the Earth; and echo sounding can be used to measure the depth of water at sea.

6 An ultrasound pulse is being used to measure the thickness of a metal beam. An ultrasonic transmitter is connected to an oscilloscope and a single pulse in sent into the beam. The speed of sound in the metal is 2000 m/s. The trace produced is shown in this diagram.

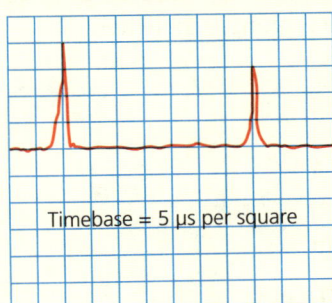

Timebase = 5 µs per square

a Use the information to calculate the thickness of the metal coating. `3 marks`

b Add a line to the trace showing what you would expect to see if there was a crack inside the metal beam. `1 marks`

Questions marked **1** **1** are for GCSE Physics students only

45

7 This diagram shows two types of seismic waves passing though the different layers of the Earth.

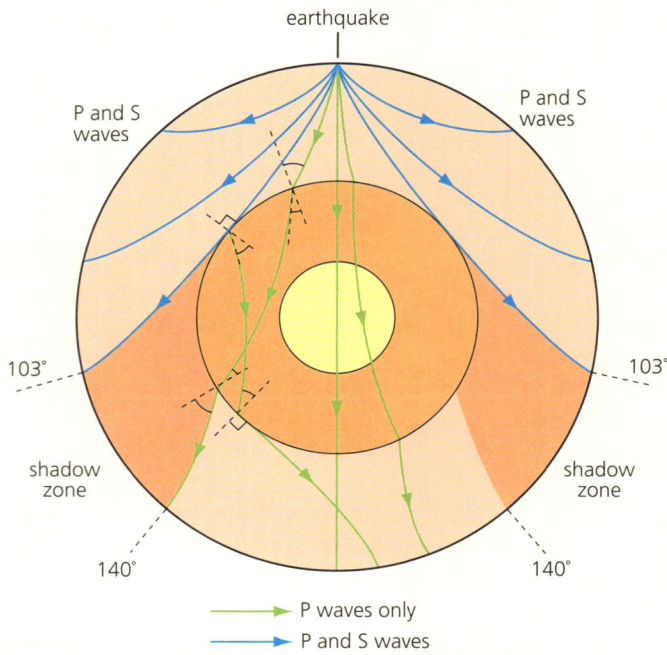

- P waves only
- P and S waves

a Label the crust, solid mantle, solid inner core and liquid outer core on the diagram. **4 marks**

b Explain what is happening to the P-waves as they reach the boundaries between the layers. **1 mark**

....

....

c Why can't P-waves pass through the outer core? **1 mark**

....

....

Electromagnetic waves

Types of electromagnetic waves

All electromagnetic waves are transverse. They form a continuous spectrum from very high frequencies to very low, falling into seven different regions. Our eyes can only detect just one of these regions, visible light.

8 a What two things do all electromagnetic waves have in common? **2 marks**

1. ....

2. ....

b The table below shows the regions of the electromagnetic spectrum.

Fill in the blank regions and complete the descriptions of wavelength and frequency. **7 marks**

.... wavelength					.... wavelength	
radio waves		infrared			X-rays	gamma rays
.... frequency				.... frequency		

Properties of electromagnetic waves 1

The behaviour of waves when they interact with different substances depends on the frequency or wavelength of the wave. Waves can refract at boundaries because of a change in their speed as they travel through different materials and this refraction can be represented by ray or wave front diagrams.

> **9** The diagram shows wave fronts moving towards a boundary – beyond which there is a more dense medium. When the waves reach the boundary, they slow down.
>
>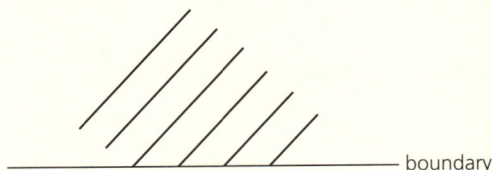
>
> a Complete the diagram to show what happens to the wave fronts after they cross the boundary. `1 mark`
>
> b Add rays to show the direction of the waves after reaching the boundary. `1 mark`

Properties of electromagnetic waves 2

Radio waves are caused by oscillating charges in electric circuit transmitters and they can cause similar oscillations in receivers far away. Gamma rays are produced by changes in the nucleus of atoms and are hazardous to living tissue when absorbed. The larger the absorbed dose (measured in sieverts) the higher the risk of damage. X-rays and ultraviolet rays can also cause damage to living tissue when absorbed.

> **10** Match the electromagnetic radiations to their source. `3 marks`
>
> | Region of spectrum | Source |
> | --- | --- |
> | Radio waves | Changes in the nucleus of an atom |
> | Gamma rays | Emitted by hot objects |
> | Infrared | Oscillating charges in electric circuits |
>
> **11** Name **two** types of electromagnetic radiation and describe the damage they can cause. `4 marks`
>
> 1. Radiation: ....
>
>   Damage: ....
>
> 2. Radiation: ....
>
>   Damage: ....

Uses and applications of electromagnetic waves

Electromagnetic waves have a wide range of uses, such as transmitting television signals, satellite communications, causing heating, sun tanning, and for medical treatment and medical imaging. Different regions of the spectrum are used for these different applications.

Waves

Questions marked 1 1 are for GCSE Physics students only

47

12 Connect the wave regions to their typical applications. `6 marks`

Region of spectrum	Typical uses
Radio waves	Electrical heating, thermal imaging
Microwaves	Fibre optic communications
Infrared	Medical imaging and treatment
Visible light	Television and radio transmissions
Ultraviolet	Satellite communication and cooking food
X-rays and gamma rays	Sun tanning, fluorescent lamps

Lenses

Lenses refract light and form images. These images have different properties depending on the type of lens used and the position of the object the light is coming from. Ray diagrams can be used to explain how an image is formed and its properties.

13 Complete the ray diagram for this object (the left-hand arrow). The object and the image have been drawn for you. `3 marks`

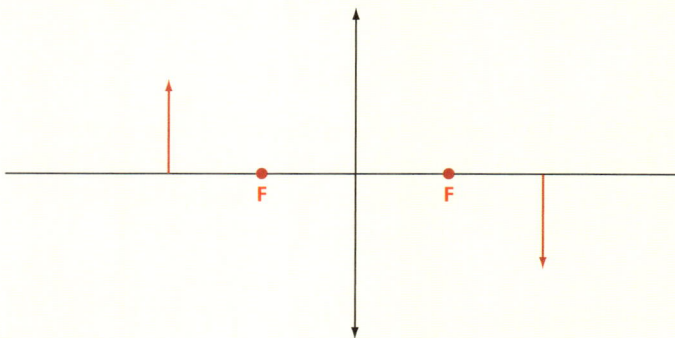

14 State the properties of the image formed. `3 marks`

....

Visible light

Visible light is only a small part of the electromagnetic spectrum and it is split into seven different colour regions. The colour of an object will depend on the colours of light hitting it and which of those colours it reflects or absorbs. Colour filters allow some parts of the visible spectrum through but absorb other parts.

15 Use colours to complete this diagram showing transmission and reflection of coloured light. `6 marks`

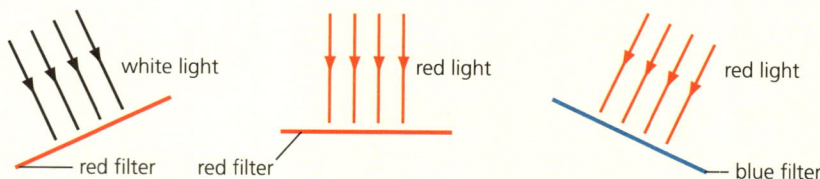

white light — red filter   red filter — red light   red light — blue filter

red object   white object   blue object

Questions marked **1** **1** are for Combined Science Trilogy and GCSE Physics students

Black body radiation

Emission and absorption of infrared radiation

All objects emit infrared radiation but the hotter the object is the more radiation it emits. An object that absorbs all the radiation reaching it is called a 'black body. These objects are perfect absorbers and also perfect emitters. The higher the temperature of a black body the more radiation it will emit at shorter wavelengths.

16 **Use the words below to complete the following sentences describing emission and absorption of radiation.** （5 marks）

black bodies　　temperature　　emitters　　radiation　　wavelength

The best possible surfaces for the absorption of .... are called

....

These absorb all the radiation that reaches them and are also the best possible

....

of radiation. The intensity and .... of the radiation emitted by a black body

depends on the ....

17 **The two curves on the graph on the right show the radiation emitted by the same object at two different temperatures.**

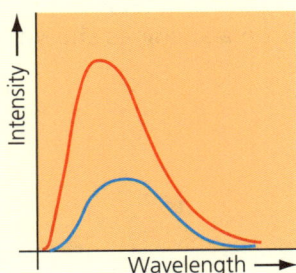

a　Label the curves as 'L' for the lower temperature and 'H' for the higher temperature. （2 marks）

b　Which object was emitting the most radiation overall? （1 mark）

....

c　Explain your answer to part b. （1 mark）

....

....

Perfect black body radiation

When an object emits more radiation than it absorbs, it cools down. When it absorbs more than it emits, it heats up. When emission and absorption are balanced, the temperature remains the same. The Earth absorbs and emits radiation and its temperature will change if it absorbs more than it emits, or vice versa.

Questions marked 🔵 🔴 are for GCSE Physics students only

49

Waves

18 The diagram below is a simplified diagram showing the absorption and emission of radiation by the Earth.

`6 marks`

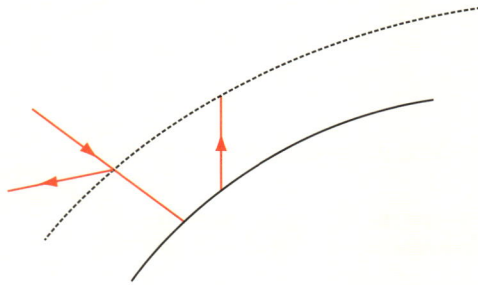

Add the following labels to the diagram.

- radiation emitted by the Sun
- radiation reflected by the atmosphere
- radiation passes through the atmosphere
- radiation is absorbed by the surface of the Earth
- longer wavelength radiation is emitted from the surface of the Earth
- longer wavelength radiation absorbed by gases in the atmosphere

Exam-style questions

🕙 10

19 During an experiment a student uses a vibrating source to produce waves on a string as shown in the diagram. The frequency of the source is 300 Hz.

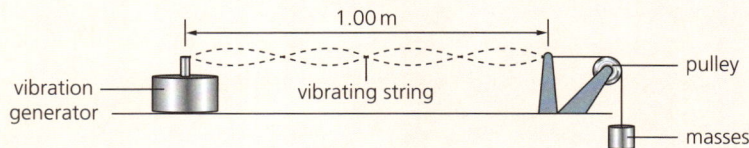

a Tick (✓) the box indicating the type of waves shown. `1 mark`

☐ Transverse waves ☐ Longitudinal waves

b What is the wavelength of the wave? `1 mark`

....

c Calculate the speed of the waves travelling in the string. `2 marks`

....

....

20 A student puts an object near a convex lens as shown in this diagram.

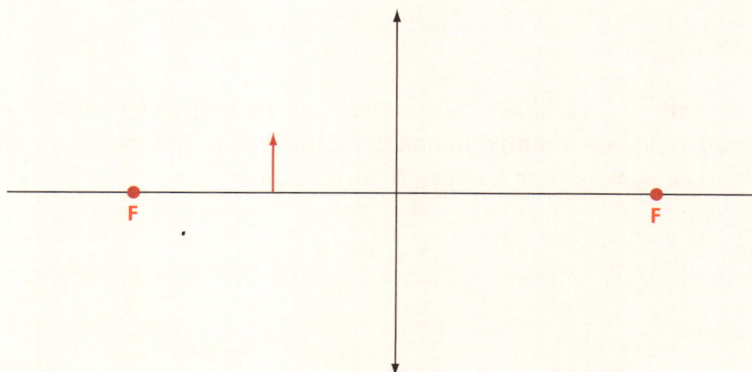

Questions marked ❶ ❶ are for Combined Science Trilogy and GCSE Physics students

a   Complete this ray diagram to show the position of the image.   `3 marks`

b   Describe the three properties of the image produced.   `3 marks`

....

c   With a different lens the student measures an object size of 12.0 cm and an image size of 30 cm.

Calculate the magnification produced by this lens.   `1 mark`

....

....

Magnetism and electromagnetism

Permanent and induced magnetism, magnetic forces and fields

Magnets interact with other magnets through the magnetic fields that surround them. Permanent magnets produce their own magnetic fields while induced magnets are only magnetic when placed near another magnet. Magnets have two poles, called the north and south poles. Poles that are similar (e.g. north and north) will repel each other but opposite poles will attract each other.

Poles of a magnet

1 The diagram below shows three possible combinations of magnets.

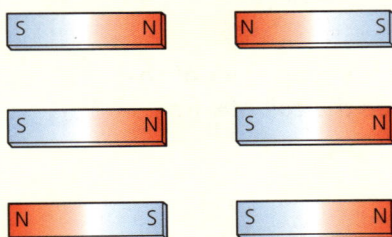

| S   N | | N   S |

| S   N | | S   N |

| N   S | | S   N |

a   Draw force arrows to show whether the magnets would be attracting each other or repelling each other.   `3 marks`

b   There is only one more possible combination. Draw this and show the forces acting.   `1 mark`

2 The diagram below shows a bar magnet holding three steel paper clips.

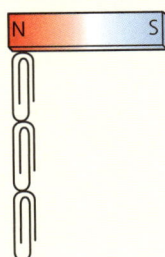

| N   S |

a   Label the permanent and induced magnets on the diagram.   `1 mark`

b   Label the north and south poles on the paper clips.   `3 marks`

c   What will happen to the magnetism of the paper clips when they are removed from the magnet?   `1 mark`

Questions marked **1** **1** are for GCSE Physics students only

51

3. Sketch the shape of the field around this permanent bar magnet. Make sure you show the direction of the field.

N [   ] S

2 marks

4. Describe **one** method of showing the shape of this field in an experiment.

1 mark

....

....

The motor effect

Electromagnetism

A current in a wire will produce a circular magnetic field around the wire at right angles to it. Wrapping the wire into a coil, called a solenoid, will increase the strength of the magnetic field. The field around the solenoid is similar in shape to the field around a bar magnet, but the field continues inside the coil where it becomes strong and uniform. Solenoids are used in electromagnets.

5. Describe how the magnetic field around a current-carrying wire can be demonstrated. 1 mark

6. The diagram below shows the field surrounding a solenoid.

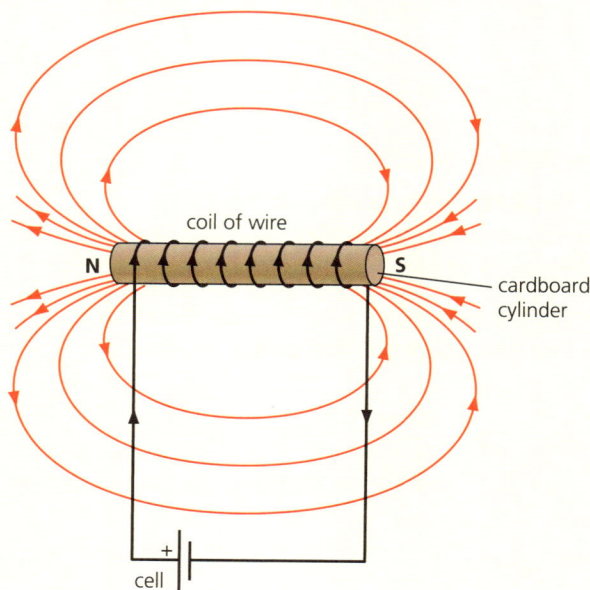

coil of wire

N   S

cardboard cylinder

+
cell

a List **three** ways of increasing the strength of this field. 3 marks

1. ....

2. ....

3. ....

b Describe the properties of the field inside the coil of wire. 2 marks

....

....

....

....

Fleming's left-hand rule

Fleming's left-hand rule describes the relationship between the force acting on a conductor, the current flowing in it and the magnetic field around it. All three of these act at right angles to each other. The size of the force acting on a current carrying wire is calculated using:

force = magnetic flux density × current × length

$F = B I l$

Questions marked 🔵 🟠 are for Combined Science Trilogy and GCSE Physics students

7 The diagram shows a left hand being used to determine the direction of the force acting on a wire. The second finger (current) has been labelled. Label the first finger and the thumb.

2 marks

seCond finger :
Current

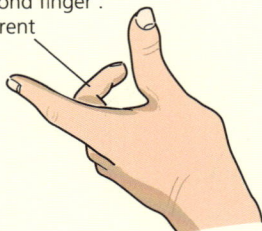

8 Match the quantities in the table with their correct units by drawing lines to join them.

4 marks

Force		tesla (T)
Current		newton (N)
Magnetic flux density		metre (m)
Length		ampere (A)

9 Calculate the force acting on these two wires:

a a wire of length 0.30 m carrying a current of 0.20 A perpendicular to a magnetic field of 5.0 mT

2 marks

....

....

b a wire of length 0.25 m carrying a current of 4.0 mA in a magnetic field of 6.5 μT   **2 marks**

....

....

Electric motors

An electric motor uses the motor effect to produce rotation. The two sides of the coil feel forces in opposite directions and this creates a moment around the axle, which gives this turning effect.

The diagram shows an electric motor.

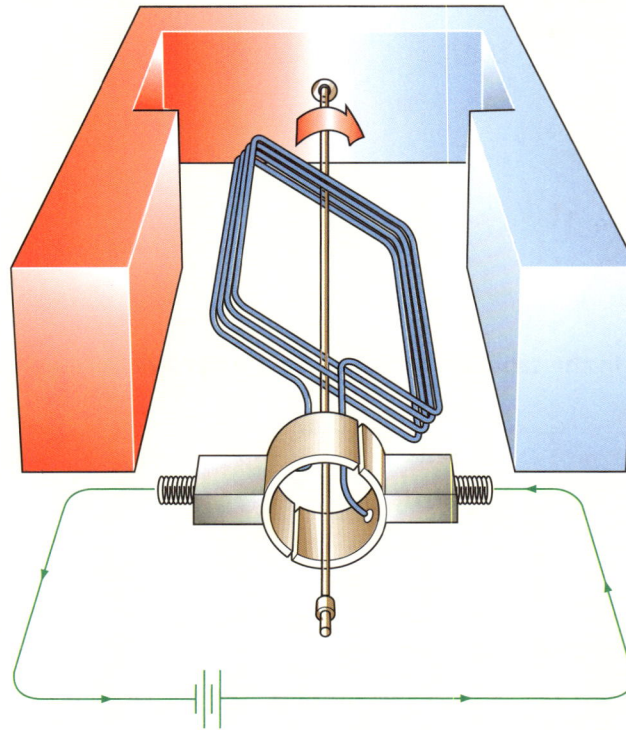

10 Add the following labels to the diagram.

5 marks

pivot   coil   carbon brushes   split-ring commutator   magnet

11 Explain why the motor rotates when a current passes through the coil.

5 marks

....

....

....

....

12 What is the purpose of the split-ring commutator?

2 marks

....

....

13 List three things you can do to increase the force of the motor.

3 marks

....

....

Loudspeakers

Loudspeakers use the motor effect to convert a varying electrical signal into vibrations in the air. The current in the wire makes the coil become an electromagnet and this interacts with the permanent magnet to create a changing force on the coil.

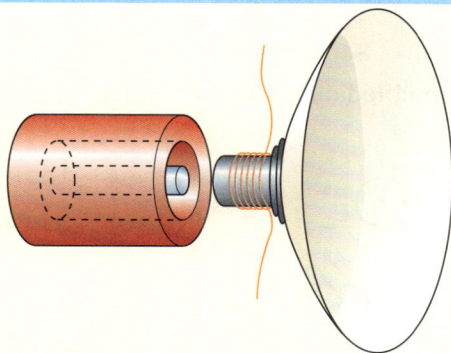

14 Add the following labels to the diagram. **3 marks**

coil   paper cone   cylinder magnet

15 Describe how the loudspeaker converts an electrical signal into a sound wave. **4 marks**

....

....

....

....

Induced potential, transformers and the National Grid

Induced potential

16 Use some of the words below to complete the sentence describing induction. **3 marks**

circuit   insulator   conductor   resistance   potential difference

When an electrical .... moves through a magnetic field, a ....

.... is induced between the ends of the conductor. Connecting the conductor

in a .... will produce a current.

17 This diagram shows a wire being moved between two magnets. The wire is connected to an ammeter.

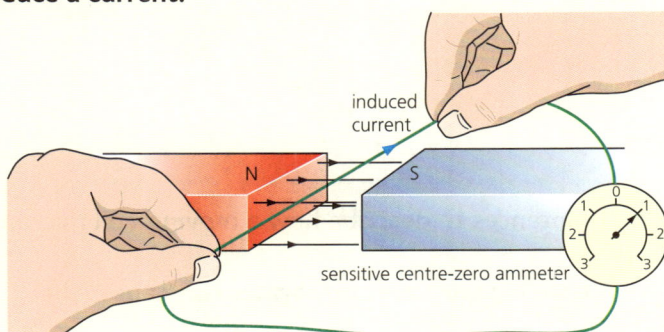

induced current

N   S

sensitive centre-zero ammeter

a Which of the following changes will increase the size of the induced potential difference? Tick (✓) all that are correct. **2 marks**

☐ Increasing the strength of the magnetic field by using stronger magnets

☐ Reversing the direction of movement

☐ Moving the wire more quickly

b Which of the following changes will reverse the direction of the current in the wire? **2 marks**

☐ Moving the wire more quickly

☐ Reversing the direction of movement

☐ Reversing the direction of the magnets

Questions marked **1** **1** are for GCSE Physics students only

Uses of the generator effect

18 The diagrams below show a simplified dynamo and the oscilloscope trace produced when it is working.

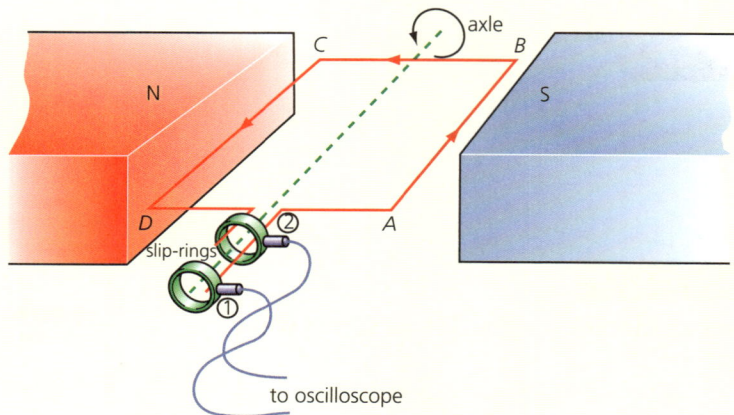

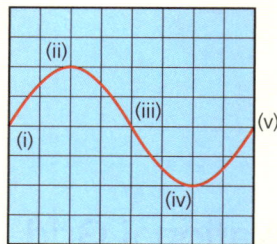

a   Describe how the oscilloscope trace will change when the dynamo coil is rotated faster.   **2 marks**

....

....

b   What is the purpose of the split-ring commutator?   **1 mark**

....

....

Microphones

19 Complete the sentences to describe how a moving-coil microphone operates.   **3 marks**

Sound waves cause a paper cone to vibrate. This causes the .... of

the microphone to vibrate. The coil moves through the magnetic field produced by the

.... magnet and this induces a ....

in the coil.

Transformers

Transformers are devices used to change the potential difference of an alternating source. They are made using two coils of wire wrapped around an iron core. A step-down transformer decreases the pd and a step-up transformer increases the pd. The relationship between the potential differences and the number of coils on the transformer is:

$$\frac{V_\text{p}}{V_\text{s}} = \frac{N_\text{p}}{N_\text{s}}$$

Changing the potential difference also changes the current (I) – for a 100% efficient transformer:

$$V_\text{s} \times I_\text{s} = V_\text{p} \times I_\text{p}$$

20 This flowchart explains the operation of a step-up transformer connected to an output circuit. Number the boxes in the correct order. **4 marks**

Stage:	Stage:	Stage:	Stage: ....
The alternating current causes an alternating magnetic field in the iron core.	The alternating potential difference produces an alternating electric current in the secondary circuit.	The alternating magnetic field induces an alternating potential difference in the secondary coil.	An alternating current is applied to the primary (input) coil.

21 Use the transformer equation to complete this table. **8 marks**

Primary potential difference	Number of turns on primary coil	Secondary potential difference	Number of turns on secondary coil	Step-up (U) or step-down (D)?
V_p	N_p	V_s	N_s	—
230 V	2000		100	
110 V		11 V	300	
500 V	4000	2.5 kV		
	50	42 V	750	

22 A transformer has 200 turns in its primary coil and 1200 on its output coil. The alternating current in the input coil is 35 mA.

a What is the current in the secondary coil? **2 marks**

....

....

b What would happen to the current if the transformer was less than 100% efficient? **1 mark**

....

....

c What would happen to the current in the secondary coil if a direct current were used? **1 mark**

....

....

Exam-style questions

23 A transformer at a power station has 500 turns on its primary coil. It changes the alternating potential difference from 20 kV to 250 000 V. The current into the transformer is 150 A.

   a Calculate the number of turns on the primary coil. `2 marks`

   ....

   ....

   b Calculate the current in the secondary coil of the transformer. `2 marks`

   ....

   ....

   c What assumption is made to answer part **b**? `1 mark`

   ....

24 A student is trying to determine the strength of the magnetic field produced by a pair of magnets. They place the pair of magnets in a frame on top of a balance as shown in the diagram below. The student measures the length of the wire inside the field and the weight of the magnets and frame. They then connect the wire to a circuit and pass a current though it. The weight shown on the balance decreases.

Length of wire 15 cm, current 2.4 A, weight without current 3.40 N, weight with current 3.38 N

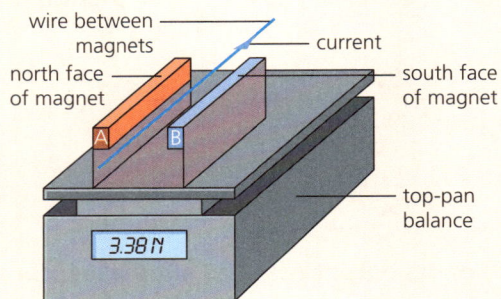

   a Explain why the apparent weight of the frame and magnets decreases when a current flows in the wire. `3 marks`

   ....

   ....

   ....

   b What is the direction of the magnetic field. Tick (✓) the correct answer. `1 mark`

   ☐ from A to B   ☐ from B to A

   c Calculate the strength of the magnetic field between the magnets. `2 marks`

   ....

   ....

Questions marked 🔵 🟠 are for Combined Science Trilogy and GCSE Physics students

25 This diagram shows a single loop of wire coil placed in a magnetic field. A current is passed through the coil in the direction shown.

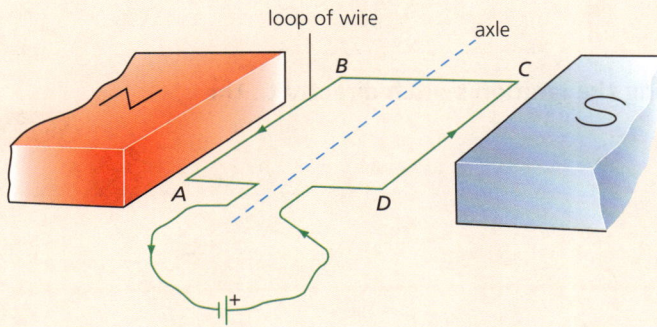

a What is the direction of the force acting on the side of the loop marked A B? `1 mark`

....

b What is the direction of the force acting on the side of the loop marked C D? `1 mark`

....

c Give one way that the direction of rotation of the motor could be reversed. `1 mark`

....

d Give three things that can increase the size of the force acting on the coil in a motor. `3 marks`

....

....

26 The diagram below shows a relay circuit in a car. The relay is used to operate a starter motor that requires a current of 100 A.

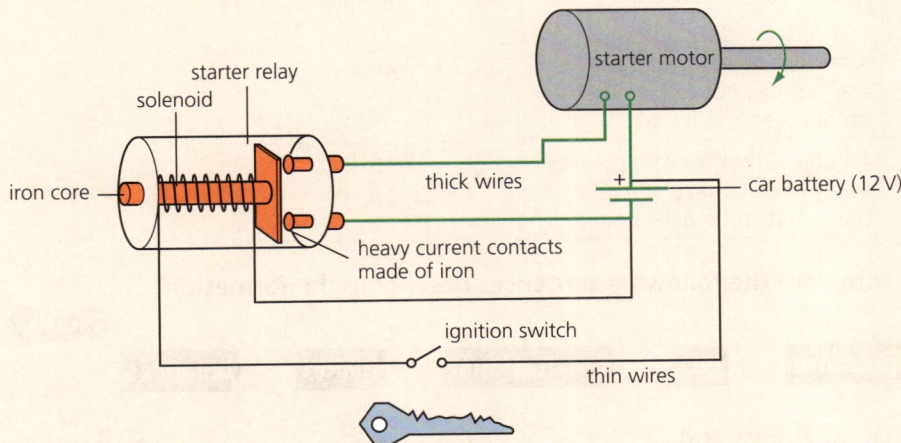

a What happens to the solenoid when the ignition switch is closed? `1 mark`

....

b How does the solenoid turn on the starter motor? `2 marks`

....

....

c Why is a relay used instead of connecting the ignition switch directly to the starter motor? `1 mark`

....

....

Space physics
Solar system, stability of orbital motions, satellites
Our solar system

Our solar system consists of a star and the objects in orbit around it along with the objects that orbit them. There are many other solar systems with similar structures spread throughout the vast collection of stars in our galaxy, the Milky Way. Stars form when clouds of gas and dust collapse and the pressures caused by gravitational forces start to compress nuclei together.

1 Match each object to the purpose of that component; and then to an example. `10 marks`

Object		Purpose		Example
A star		A very large object found in the centre of a solar system.		Jupiter
A planet		A vast collection of billions of stars held together by gravitational forces.		The Milky Way
A moon		A large object that orbits a star.		The Sun
A dwarf planet		A smaller object that orbits a star but has not removed the other objects in its orbit.		Europa
A galaxy		An object that orbits a planet – many planets have several of these, but some have none.		Pluto

2 Use the words below to complete the following sentences describing the formation of a star. `7 marks`

stable   nebula   pressure   gas   gravitational   fusion   balances

A star is formed when a cloud of dust and .... (a ....) is pulled

together by .... forces. The particles form a sphere, which gradually decreases

in size. The .... inside the star increases as it shrinks and is eventually high

enough to force small nuclei tighter in .... reactions. Once these reactions

start they produce an outwards pressure which .... the force of gravity pulling

inwards. The star is then ....

Questions marked **1** **1** are for Combined Science Trilogy and GCSE Physics students

Orbital motion, natural and artificial satellites

The planets orbit a sun because the force of the sun's gravity acts on them and is causing them to constantly change direction (accelerate). They follow almost circular paths around the sun. Moons orbit their planets due to the gravitational forces from those planets.

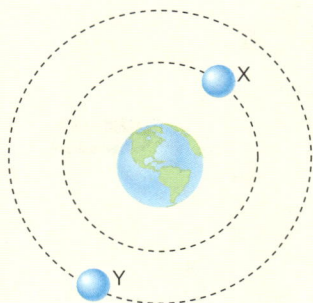

3 This diagram shows a pair of moons in orbit around a planet.

a Draw force arrows to show the gravitational forces acting. **2 marks**

b Which moon will have the highest speed? **1 mark**

....

c Explain your answer to part b. **1 mark**

....

....

The life cycle of a star

Stars do not stay the same forever. They go through a 'life cycle' during which their appearance and behaviour change dramatically. At different points in this process, stars fuse together small nuclei and make larger ones; this is the origin of most of the elements in the universe. The heaviest elements are formed when stars explode in a supernova.

4 The flowchart below shows the life cycle of our Sun. Complete the diagram by adding the life cycle of a star that is much larger than our Sun. **4 marks**

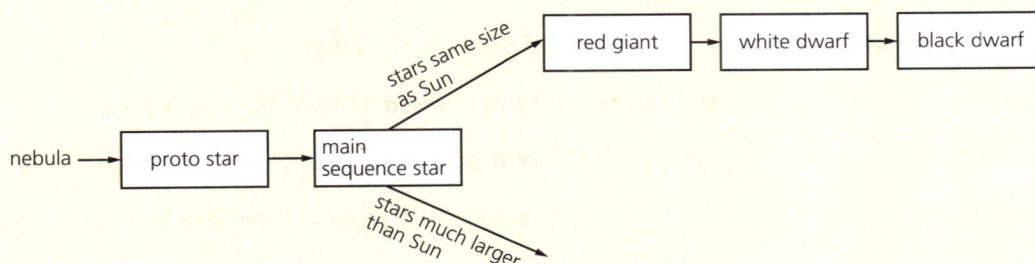

nebula → proto star → main sequence star

stars same size as Sun → red giant → white dwarf → black dwarf

stars much larger than Sun →

5 Complete this table to describe the processes which are happening at each stage of a star's life. **6 marks**

Name of stage	Description
	The star is hot, but no fusion reactions are happening yet.
	All reactions in the star have stopped. The star no longer gives out radiation.
	Fusion reactions produce a pressure that balances the gravitational attraction.
	The outer layers of the star have escaped leaving the incredible hot core.
Red giant / Red supergiant	
Supernova	
	The star has collapsed and become so dense that the gravitational field is so strong that not even light can escape.
	The core of the star collapses so that electrons are forced into protons leaving a very dense material made of only neutrons.

6 Elements are produced in stars during different phases of their life cycle.

  a For the three elements below indicate whether they were formed during the main sequence of a star (M), a supernova explosion (S) or were not produced in a star at all (N). `3 marks`

Carbon	Hydrogen	Gold

  b Explain how the gold produced in stars ended up on Earth. `2 marks`

....

....

Red-shift

When we observe light from distant galaxies we see that the wavelength of the light increases with distance. This effect is called red-shift. This indicates that the galaxies are moving away from us. The further away they are the faster they are receding. The red-shift of galaxies supports the Big Bang theory, that the universe began as a very small and very dense region.

7 Use some of the words below to complete the following sentence. `7 marks`

matter   hot   cold   red-shift   faster   slower

density   expanded   contracted   universe   solar system

The Big Bang theory suggests that the .... began as a very small region of

space which was extremely .... and dense. This region ....

rapidly and the .... and temperature decreased. One of the key pieces of

evidence for this is the .... of different galaxies which shows that the further

away the galaxy is the .... it is travelling. This supports the idea that all of the

.... in the universe was once much closer together than it is now.

8 The graph below shows the speeds at which distant galaxies are moving away from us compared to their distance. The distances are measured in a very large unit called the megaparsec (Mpc).

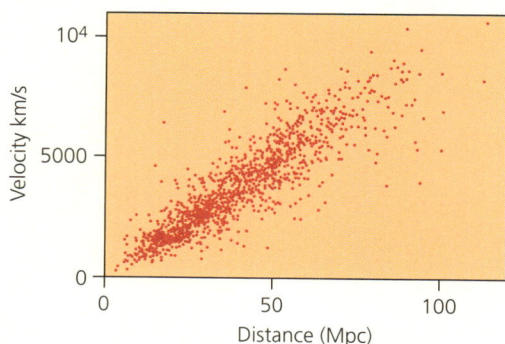

  a Describe the relationship between the distance and the velocity. `1 mark`

....

....

Questions marked **1** **1** are for Combined Science Trilogy and GCSE Physics students

b Explain how this evidence supports the Big Bang theory. **3 marks**

....

....

....

....

Exam-style questions

⏱ **15**

9 Our star, the Sun, is in the main sequence phase of its life cycle.

a Explain why the Sun remains a constant size and at a constant temperature during the main sequence phase of its life. **4 marks**

....

....

....

....

b Describe the processes that will happen to the Sun after it leaves the main sequence. **6 marks**

....

....

....

....

....

10 The light from a galaxy can be analysed to measure its speed as it moves in the universe. If a galaxy is moving, then the spectrum of the light detected is different from the spectrum of a galaxy that is not moving. The diagram below shows the spectrum emitted by our Sun (upper) compared to the spectrum from a distant galaxy (lower).

Shorter wavelength (higher frequency)   Longer wavelength (lower frequency)

400 nm   500   600   700

a Explain the difference between the two spectra. `3 marks`

....

....

....

b The Big Bang theory is a scientific theory to describe the evolution of the universe. Use some of the words below to complete the description of the Big Bang theory and the evidence for it. `4 marks`

| hot | cold | contracted | expanded | slower |
| faster | millions | billions | small | large |

The Big Bang theory suggests that the universe started from a very ....

region which was extremely .... and dense. From this initial state the

universe .... rapidly.

Red-shift observations show that the further a galaxy is away from us the

.... it is moving. This shows that .... of years ago the

galaxies were all much closer together.

Hachette UK's policy is to use papers that are natural, renewable and recyclable products and made from wood grown in sustainable forests. The logging and manufacturing processes are expected to conform to the environmental regulations of the country of origin.

Orders: please contact Bookpoint Ltd, 130 Park Drive, Milton Park, Abingdon, Oxon OX14 4SE. Telephone: (44) 01235 827827. Fax: (44) 01235 400401. Email education@bookpoint.co.uk Lines are open from 9 a.m. to 5 p.m., Monday to Saturday, with a 24-hour message answering service. You can also order through our website: www.hoddereducation.co.uk

ISBN 978-1-5104-1905-6

© Darren Forbes 2018

First published in 2018 by
Hodder Education,
An Hachette UK company
Blenheim Court
George Street
Banbury
Oxfordshire OX16 5BH

www.hoddereducation.co.uk

Impression number   10 9 8 7 6 5 4 3 2 1

Year   2022 2021 2020 2019 2018

Cover photo © Mark Penny/Fotolia

Typeset by Aptara, India

Printed in Spain

A catalogue record for this title is available from the British Library.

HODDER EDUCATION

t: 01235 827827

e: education@bookpoint.co.uk

w: hoddereducation.co.uk

ISBN 978-1-5104-1905-6

9 781510 419056

MIX
Paper from
responsible sources
FSC C104740